FLORENCE OF AMERICA

University of Regina Press designates one title each year that best exemplifies the guiding editorial and manuscript production principles of long-time senior editor Donna Grant.

Florence *of* America

A Feminist in the Age of McCarthyism

Florence Bean James
with Jean Freeman

Printed and bound in Canada at Friesens. The text of this book is printed on 100% post-consumer recycled paper with earth-friendly vegetable-based inks.

Cover and text design: Duncan Campbell, University of Regina Press
Copy editor: Marionne Cronin
Proofreader: Nadine Coderre

Cover and frontispiece photo: "Florence James being escorted out of the Canwell Committee hearing." MOHAI, *Seattle Post-Intelligencer* Collection, 1986.5.30003.1

Library and Archives Canada Cataloguing in Publication

Title: Florence of America : a feminist in the age of McCarthyism / Florence Bean James ; with Jean Freeman.

Other titles: Fists upon a star

Names: James, Florence Bean, 1892–1988, author. | Freeman, Jean, 1934– author.

Series: Regina collection ; 12.

Description: Series statement: The Regina collection ; 12 | Originally published as Fists upon a star : a memoir of love, theatre, and escape from McCarthyism, by University of Regina Press, Regina, Saskatchewan, ©2013.

Identifiers: Canadiana (print) 20190110694 | Canadiana (ebook) 20190110708 | ISBN 9780889776470 (hardcover) | ISBN 9780889776487 (PDF) | ISBN 9780889776494 (HTML)

Subjects: LCSH: James, Florence Bean, 1892-1988. | LCSH: James, Florence Bean, 1892-1988,—Exile,—Saskatchewan. | LCSH: Theatrical producers and directors,—United States,—Biography. | LCSH: Feminists,—United States,—Biography. | LCSH: Theater,—United States,—History,—20th century. | LCSH: [Anti-communist movements,—United States,—History,—20th century. | LCGFT: Autobiographies.

Classification: LCC PN2287.J34 A3 2019 | DDC 792.02/33092,—dc23

University of Regina Press

Saskatchewan, Canada, S4S 0A2
tel: (306) 585-4758 fax: (306) 585-4699
web: www.uofrpress.ca

10 9 8 7 6 5 4 3 2 1

We acknowledge the support of the Canada Council for the Arts for our publishing program. We acknowledge the financial support of the Government of Canada. / Nous reconnaissons l'appui financier du gouvernement du Canada. This publication was made possible through Creative Saskatchewan's Creative Industries Production Grant Program.

Canada Council for the Arts Conseil des arts du Canada Canada creative SASKATCHEWAN

To Burton, who put my hand with his upon that star. To Marijo and Al and all the others who lived through so much of this with us. And to Jean, who finally gave me some joy in the preparation of this book.

—Florence Bean James

(October 27, 1892–January 18, 1988)

Contents

Preface

JEAN FREEMAN

Like many other people in Saskatchewan, I first heard of Florence James from my high school drama teacher, who was fresh from a class Florence and her husband, Burton (better known as "Pop"), had conducted in 1951 at the Saskatchewan Arts Board's Summer School.

Burton died on November 13, 1951, and in 1952 Florence returned to teach summer classes in Saskatchewan by herself. That summer, I signed up for her two-week session in the Qu'Appelle Valley. As a bright-eyed wannabe actor, I was mightily impressed by this forceful, knowledgeable woman. I returned to take her classes for several summers after that, even after I had graduated and moved on to community theatre.

Mrs. James (we always called her "Mrs. James" in those days) was a touch formidable—you didn't fool around in her classes. But she knew her stuff. We respected her, and we learned from her.

Many years later, in her papers, I found the letter from Arts Board Secretary Norah McCullough, inviting Florence to make her connection with the board a permanent one. The letter was dated September 11, 1952, and said that while Norah and Executive Director David Smith hadn't yet been able to present the idea to Dr. William Riddell, chairman of the board, "we are afraid you will escape us, so this is to make you aware of the possibility so you won't vanish out of our ken without contacting us en route. We think we can find $4,000 in the budget plus traveling expenses, up to September of 1953 anyway, with some work at Regina College, but most of it out on the flat. Let us know if we should proceed. If you want to come, we want you!"

She did want to, and so she came and stayed until 1968—mostly "out on the flat."

During that time, from her late sixties into her eighties, Florence began to write a book about her life—the girlhood years that shaped her, her experiences with Burton, their time in the theatre, building the Seattle Repertory Playhouse, their tribulations, and their successes. It was the book that Burton and Bob Johnson had planned to write. Because Florence felt she wasn't really a writer, she took some writing classes from Saskatchewan author

Ken Mitchell, who was teaching at the Summer School. She wrote and rewrote and wrote some more.

In 1962, I went to work for the Saskatchewan Arts Board as a communications officer, first part-time, then full-time. My cubbyhole was next to Florence's office in a drafty porch at Saskatchewan House in Regina, the former residence of the province's Lieutenant-Governor. As the board's drama consultant, however, she spent most of her time criss-crossing the province, in fair weather and foul, to stimulate theatre of the people, by the people, and for the people, in the province she loved so much.

Florence made no secret of the fact that she was amazed at being paid—she thought even lavishly paid compared to what she'd received during her many years at the Repertory Playhouse in Seattle—to do something she enjoyed.

On one of her stops back at home base, she told me about the book she was trying to write and asked if I could help organize some of the material. I did, and she asked if I would do some editing. Then she suggested I might rewrite things here and there, and, finally, she asked me to write some portions of the book and pull it all together.

I was glad to help, honoured by her trust and confidence in my ability and by her growing closeness as a friend. We worked on the manuscript regularly over the following years. When Florence felt it contained what she wanted to say, and I felt I had done all I could do to put it into finished form, the attempt to find a publisher began. The theatre presses liked the chapters about her teaching methods and theatre experiences but not the personal bits. The women's presses liked Florence's story but felt there was too much emphasis on her husband. The regular publishers weren't interested because it wasn't mainstream. And the University of Washington Press just wasn't interested. So the manuscript went into a box and gathered dust. It was thirty years later that actress Rita Shelton Deverell, a vigorous friend of Mrs. James and an ardent champion of her achievements and life story, tempted the Canadian Plains Research Center (now University of Regina Press) to take a look.

As publication has become not just a dream but a reality, I am deeply indebted for the help of many friends, old and new, in checking and double-checking memories and details: sincere thanks to Rita Shelton Deverell, Joan McGilvray, Jim and Kathleen Kinzel and Debbie Scotton Kinzel, Kurt Armbruster, Anne Stewart, Terry Bleifuss, Donna Grant, Bruce Walsh, and University of Regina Press.

For the last years of Florence's life, as her eyesight steadily deteriorated, I became a sort of personal secretary and amanuensis, writing letters, making phone calls, reading to her—mail, papers, and hundreds of books, plays, and poems—meeting through her the myriad wonderful people who were (and are to this day) the Friends of Florence James, and at the same time enriching my own life, and that of my family, through her example.

I spent so many hours in research, discussion, and writing on the book, and in reading and rereading it to Florence and others, that I find it difficult sometimes to realize that I didn't live through those days: I never walked home from school through the sagebrush in Pocatello, Idaho; I never marched for women's suffrage through the streets of New York City, or stood charged in a court of law for standing by my guns in opposing an unconstitutional investigation, convicted of the crime of being consistent; I never had the chance to sit in a darkened theatre and listen to Woody Guthrie play a fundraiser for my Playhouse. But, through Florence, I did. I hope that, through her book, many others will also have the chance to follow Florence's steps, even if it's just in their imagination.

The book's final form is a pastiche of memoir, biography, and autobiography. It follows a general chronology for the most part, but Florence liked to drop in anecdotes or references when they occurred to her, or whenever they seemed appropriate. I did try on a few occasions to rearrange the text in order to straighten the flow, but then I realized this was the way Florence remembered the story, and told the story, so I just left it alone.

When failing eyesight put an end to Florence's work for the Arts Board, her protégé Ken Kramer provided a welcome haven for another decade as dramaturge for Regina's Globe Theatre, which she had been instrumental in founding in 1966.

Toward the end of her life, almost blind, unable to work, confined to a hospital bed, having lost her husband, her only child, and many of her closest friends, Florence would rail and rage. "Why am I still here?" she'd say. "I think the good Lord is trying to teach me patience, but I'm not a very good student!" I could never answer her question. I lamely said there had to be some purpose; it just wasn't given us to see what it was.

Some of those who remember Florence and honour her life and achievements would say that hope is her legacy. For me, it is probably patience . . . not patience in the sense of meek and quiet acceptance, but patience in the sense of relentless persistence: "Don't let the bastards wear you down. If we can't outmaneuver them, we'll outwit them and outlast them!"

Florence took her final curtain call on this stage on January 18, 1988, at the age of ninety-five, and promptly moved, I am sure, to heaven's green room, ready for the opening of the next act.

At Florence's memorial service, I read something I had never read to her, in all those thousands of hours together—but she would have loved it if I had, because it was jotted down by the actress Ellen Terry on the flyleaf of a favourite book and found after her death in 1928:

> No funeral gloom, my dears, when I am gone
> —corpse-gazings, tears, black raiment, graveyard grimness.
> Think of me as withdrawn into the dimness;
> yours still, you mine. Remember all the best
> of our past moments, and forget the rest.
> And so to where I wait, come gently on.
>
> —*William Allingham*

Editor's Introduction

SEAN PRPICK

The epic story of Florence Bean James is one that University of Regina Press is passionate about, written by one of the giants of both American and Canadian theatre.

With the help of Regina-based writer Jean Freeman, Mrs. James moves us briskly through her long career as an actor, director, and theatrical impresario, all told against the backdrop of the great events of the twentieth century.

On these pages you can read how she and her husband, Burton, first tasted theatrical success in New York City in the Roaring Twenties, with the help of young up-and-comers like Jimmy Cagney, and how they prospered by bringing cutting-edge stage performances to Seattle. After some heady early artistic triumphs on the

West Coast, the Jameses endured the Great Depression, a World War, and then, most catastrophically of all, the destruction of their careers in the infamous Red Scare of the late 1940s. It was a time of unreason and intolerance in America that has uncomfortable resonance with many living through the Trump era today.

In her time, Mrs. James had a choice of submitting or fighting this injustice, and she chose to fight. She fought to the point where she was once bodily hauled from a hearing into her supposed disloyalty to America. It's the moment captured on the front cover of this book.

Like any good play, though, life's adversities led Mrs. James to a triumphant final act. That happened when she won more honours and fresh professional success in her adopted new homeland of Canada. To our country's great and lasting benefit, she got in on the ground floor as the first arts board in the nation took shape right here in Saskatchewan under the patronage of Tommy Douglas.

Starting in 1950—pausing only briefly to mourn her husband, Burton, who passed away in 1951—she embarked on a busy thirty-plus-year career as an administrator with the Saskatchewan Arts Board, a theatrical coach, and director and founder of theatre companies. As you'll see in Rita Shelton Deverell's epilogue at the end of this book, since Florence's death in 1988, she's been fondly remembered particularly in Regina as "godmother" to Globe Theatre, which has operated professionally in the city since 1966.

We are honoured at University of Regina Press to present the story of Florence Bean James's exemplary, inspiring, and dramatic life. To us, Mrs. James was proof positive of an observation by her peer and almost exact contemporary, American theatre coach Stella Adler, who said, "The theatre was created to tell people the truth about life."

Prologue

In the ten years since I started to write this book, at the tender age of seventy-three, I have learned a number of interesting things:

- That the gestation period of a literary work is somewhat longer than that of the Indian elephant, and the birth pangs at least as severe.

- That I am no writer, but when one has a story that must be told, one does the best one can and asks for help in a loud voice.

- That pain and joy in memory may be diminished, intensified, or altered by time, but they can never be destroyed. Each of the events and attendant emotions through which I sifted and sorted to build this story has remained like a beetle or butterfly caught in amber, like beads making up the rosary of my life.

- That friends are life's one irreplaceable treasure, that help and good advice come from many sources, and that readers and editors are patient, persistent, and long-suffering people.

- And, finally, that the hardest part of telling a story is deciding where it ought to begin. I am indebted to one of the many editors who have read my manuscript for telling me, "stories, like kittens, ought to be picked up in the middle." So, with appropriate caution, that is where I will pick up mine.

—Florence James, circa 1975

Florence *of* America

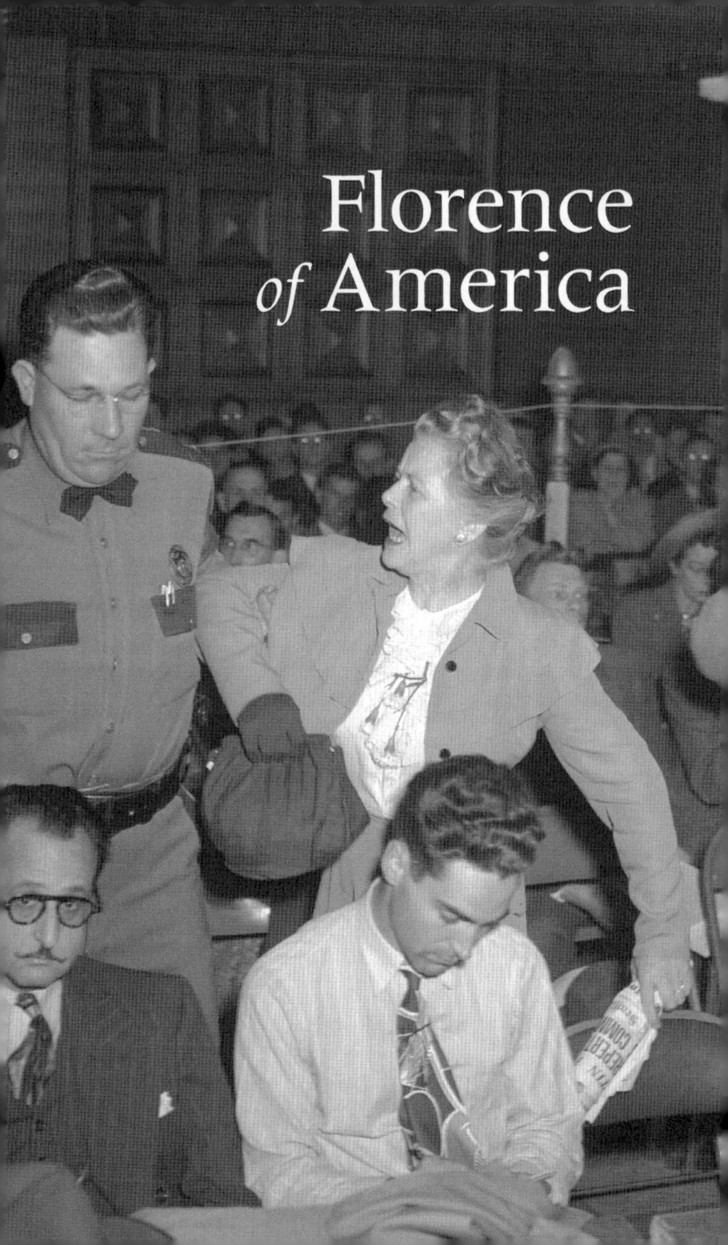

Opening Night

On a crisp evening in October 1930, the Seattle Repertory Playhouse opened the doors of its permanent home to the public—the beginning of a memorable period in the development of theatre in the regions beyond Broadway and in the state of Washington in particular. But for my husband, Burton James, and me, it was the culmination of years of planning and working toward the fulfillment of a dream—the creation of a theatre that would be more than a building, more than a star-studded roster of "hits" or "classics," more than a diversion for the social set or a job for the critics.

Burton and I had been working all our adult lives, first in New York, then in Seattle, toward a theatre that would be of the people, by the people, and for the people. Our dream had finally become reality two years before, when we launched our repertory company, with its talented, dedicated nucleus of unpaid performers.

We had worked in rented theatres, makeshift quarters, temporary facilities—but we had created a theatre. The next part of our dream was to have a proper home—and that, too, was about to come to fruition with the opening of the Seattle Repertory Playhouse on the corner of 41st and University Way, in the heart of Seattle's university district.

I can't remember what I was thinking as the clock moved inexorably toward 8:30 p.m., curtain time for George Bernard Shaw's *Major Barbara,* the production we had chosen to launch our third season and christen our new theatre. I might have thought back to the true beginning of the Seattle Repertory Playhouse—a Sunday in May 1928. Actors, students from the Cornish Players, theatre workers, and other local artists interested in founding a community theatre had come to cast their lot with ours in developing an acting-producing ensemble. We had nothing but our vitality and our faith in people, but we were determined to create a theatre in which the artist's integrity would stand above monetary considerations, a theatre that would truly belong to the community because it came from the community. In the two years since that Sunday, we felt we had made a good beginning. We had an excellent nucleus of a company, constantly augmented by new people from the community who believed as we did and were willing to work to achieve it. We had produced fifteen plays, ranging from Seán O'Casey, Henrik Ibsen, and

Luigi Pirandello to the works of three new homegrown playwrights, Garland Ethel, Albert Ottenheimer, and Marianne King.

However, in spite of our growing success with the public, our first two years were an accountant's nightmare and we operated with a constant deficit—a steadily decreasing deficit, it's true, but a deficit all the same. But we had hopes that in our own theatre, with a firm base of operation, we could eventually put the Playhouse in the black.

If I could have looked into the future that night, I would have seen no end to the red ink, which perhaps should not have come as a surprise, given the state of America's—and more particularly the theatre's—economy. But the eddies of financial disaster that rippled across the country from Wall Street's crash in 1929 were slow to reach the West Coast, and we wanted to believe that, as the politicians and the press kept telling us, prosperity lay just around the corner. We signed a ninety-nine-year lease, beginning October 1, 1930, and terminating September 30, 2029.

If I had known what lay ahead, I might have slammed the theatre doors in the faces of our arriving audience and chosen a different path. But if we hadn't gone ahead, so many good things would never have happened: excellent productions of fine plays that deserved to be done well for receptive audiences; achievements, as a group and as individuals, that would be a source of lasting pride and have far-reaching consequences; joy in the development of sensitivity and responsiveness in the thousands of people who were our audiences over the years; and, most important, proof that a theatre of the people, by the people, and for the people not only *could* live and flourish but *did*, in the perhaps improbable setting of Seattle, Washington.

I had no time that night to think of any of those things. My mind was full of the present, and it was chaotic enough to keep me fully occupied.

Eight-thirty was upon us, and we still couldn't raise the curtain. Some kind of feud was raging among the electricians, building code authorities, and the fire department and had been for months. What one approved, the others promptly disapproved. The bedlam this infighting engendered was boiling over backstage. Electricians were installing lighting equipment, and fire inspectors were haranguing over building codes. At the height of the frenzy, with the lounge and foyer crowded with patrons, spilling through the arched French windows onto the flagstone courtyard around our elm tree, an electrician accidentally set fire to the building with his blowtorch!

While Burton, in costume and full makeup, battled backstage to bring order out of chaos, I mingled with our guests, apologizing for the delay, accepting their admiring praise for the wonders our architect had wrought from an abandoned warehouse. I was dressed, as I always was for opening nights in our theatre, in a new evening gown, this time of blue crepe de Chine. I remember it was very smart—and very inexpensive. I've always felt that opening nights are occasions deserving of one's very best, so I always made sure that I had elegant dresses, but that they cost as little as possible. Our budget wouldn't permit anything else. Opening nights in our theatre were always "dress-up" occasions for our audiences too, especially in the early years.

The curtain finally rose, one hour late, and *Major Barbara* greeted the playgoers of Seattle. A deathly white glare illuminated the stage, for there had been no time to set lights or fix gels in the screens. We had no dimmer board. There were only two lighting levels that night: on and off.

Somehow, in spite of everything, the show was a success. The *Seattle Post-Intelligencer* was out front, photographing the audience with flashbulbs, then a brand-new invention replacing the old flash powder and pan. The next day, a large picture of our patrons appeared on the front page of the morning paper, alongside a review that praised the actors and gave a short history of the group's development, as well as glowing descriptions of the audience.

As we drove home that night, Burton and I were exhausted but elated. I can remember the great sense of relief that at last we were in our theatre, and that we had actually got it open. We had perhaps an inkling, but no real comprehension, of the bewildering challenges that lay ahead.

But we knew where we were going, with the brick-and-mortar fact of the building now a reality. And where we were going had been, in a very large measure, predicated by where we had come from.

Beginnings

For all of us, there are conscious and subconscious forces that prompt us to make decisions that develop into a pattern, a "habit of living." In some lives, it is fairly easy to trace the inherited or environmental pressures that create such patterns. From my vantage point in time, it is easy to identify the pressures that shaped my husband, Burton Wakeley James, and me, Mary Florence Bean James, and led to our lives taking the course they did.

Perhaps the greatest influence when I was young was my mother's attitude toward education. She craved it, revered it, and coveted it, although she never quite achieved it. My mother's parents, Thomas and Mary Hayney Lynch, were Irish immigrants. They settled in Cleveland in 1869 when Mother was five, and my grandfather worked on the iron ore docks as a day labourer. He was completely illiterate until after he married my grandmother, who had some education, having been put in an orphanage after her parents died within a few days of each other during the potato famine in the 1840s. She taught my grandfather to read, but he never succeeded in writing more than his own name.

The family moved to Nebraska around 1878, when Mother was not quite fourteen. They homesteaded a few miles from Lincoln and my mother spent her girlhood in a sod house. There was no school in their district, so her education came to an abrupt end, something she regretted all her life. But she didn't give up. She was sure there must be a way to get the education she felt was the most important thing in life. In her late teens, she decided to strike out on her own. One day, she was in Lincoln with her father when she heard that the hotel, and its manager, Mr. Criley, would like to staff its dining room with waitresses, if it could get them, to replace its Black waiters. When her father left, my shy mother said, "Mr. Criley, I'd like to be a waitress, if I could learn how to do it."

Mr. Criley agreed that, if she could recruit enough of her friends to staff the dining room, he would pay them three dollars a week, plus board and room. Delighted with the idea of making so much money, which she could then save, to go to school, she went back to the farm and recruited a number of her friends.

Remembering my mother's unassertive nature and strict Irish Catholic upbringing, I have never ceased to wonder at her determination and audacity. In those days, well-brought-up girls left the parental roof before marriage only in cases of dire necessity. But Mother's desire for an education spurred her on.

One spring day, Mr. Criley announced he was going to manage a hotel at a summer resort in Soda Springs, Idaho. Would the girls from the dining room like to come with him, just for the summer? The girls were delighted.

Before the summer at Soda Springs was over, Mr. Criley was offered the managership of the railroad hotel in the newly formed town of Pocatello, Idaho, and asked the girls if they wanted to go with him. At that point there was nothing in Pocatello but the railroad shop, a few houses the railroad had built along its one street, and the railroad hotel.

Mother and the girls decided to take the adventure being offered them and went with Mr. Criley. Mother said the girls were so homesick after a short while in the little frontier town that when boxcars marked "Omaha" came through the station, they'd rush out on the platform and kiss them! But then my father came to town, and Mother's homesickness vanished, as did her long-cherished dream of getting an education.

The man who was to become my father was the youngest son of James and Harriet Harvey Bean, English immigrants who settled in West Medford, Massachusetts, a little out of Boston. In England they had been servants on an estate—Grandfather a gardener, and

Grandmother a meat cook. They realized the only future their children could hope for in England would be in the servant class, so they immigrated to America, seeking better opportunities for them. They prospered, and my father, the youngest, was given an education and graduated from the Massachusetts Institute of Technology.

Following Horace Greeley's admonition, "Go west, young man, go west," Father and his brother James, who was a doctor, went west as far as Pocatello, where Father went to work in the railroad shop. He was also the Pocatello postmaster on a part-time basis.

Father and his brother were batching somewhere in town, but they took their meals at the hotel, and before long Mary Lynch had become engaged to Ben Bean and had to go back home to Nebraska to tell her parents. They were horrified. In 1890, it was a shocking step for an Irish Catholic to marry an English Protestant—and her not even in the family way!

I was the eldest child in the family, born on October 27, in 1892, when Mother was twenty-eight. Mother had my sister Harriet eleven months after I was born, and Grace eleven months after Harriet. Later, she lost a baby boy and, when I was ten, had Ruth, who died of influenza in 1919 when she was sixteen. James, the final child in the family, arrived when I was eleven.

I went first to Pocatello Public School and then to the Academy of Idaho, now the university. I loved going there, although it meant I had to walk a mile and a quarter through the sagebrush. After school, I would wait until my chattering classmates left so I could walk home alone, with the pink snow in winter, the smell of the sagebrush in spring and fall.

When I was a child, I remember seeing what we called the "old Indian stones." Near the Portneuf River, there were more than six acres of these lava stones, covered with pictographs. When the Pocatello Library was being built, Dr. Minnie Howard had tried to get the authorities to place some of the stones in the basement of the building, so that at least a few of them would be preserved. It wasn't done and the stones were eventually smashed to make foundations for houses being built near the river. Years later, the Smithsonian Institute sent someone out to ask about the stones, but all that was left for them to see were Dr. Howard's photographs and two stones in her fireplace.

As I look back on my childhood, it seems to have been pleasant enough to have been a child on the frontier in those days. We were brought up as ladies, of course, in dress, language, and behaviour. Our upbringing was not permissive, but we were permitted lots of things, as long as they fit the pattern of ladylike behaviour.

We always had music in our home, because Mother had a lovely, untrained voice and loved to sing. I didn't inherit my mother's voice, but I did inherit her love of music and the feeling there were things in life worth having besides the ones you could touch and hold.

Mother's feelings were a nice counterpoint to Father's, which were very much concerned with things that could be touched and held, because he was turning himself into a successful businessman. Early in the 1890s, he and some of his friends set up a hardware store, which he managed, ultimately buying out his partners. He sold stoves and heaters, and when people began installing central heating, he set up what we called a "tin shop" to make the parts necessary for the installations.

Father also sold bicycles and had an early faith in the future of the automobile, becoming Ford's agent for that northwestern area. The day Father's first Ford car arrived, he took it into the carriage house of the barn and dismantled it completely, with my brothers and sisters and me permitted to stand in the doorway and watch the process. He had to know not only how the thing ran but also why.

Eventually, Father built a garage, the only garage able to service cars between Ogden, Utah, and Butte, Montana. He also dabbled in farming and bought forty acres right outside town at ten dollars an acre, hired some Chinese people to work the farm, and grew the Idaho potato, which was just being introduced then.

With all his enterprises, it was perhaps inevitable that Father would go into politics. He was mayor of Pocatello for three terms. Losses in 1922 damaged his hard-earned fortunes, and the 1929 stock market crash wiped him out. But, when I was in my teens, he was well able to afford the tuition to send his eldest daughter to the Academy of Idaho, a kindness that was to have a profound effect on the rest of my life, for it was at the academy that I met a very special teacher, who was the single most decisive factor in turning me toward a career in the theatre.

Miss Alice Daly had her degree from the University of Minnesota and was a graduate of the Emerson College of Oratory in Boston. She must have had more than a touch of the pioneering spirit to have come to teach in this rather new institution in a frontier town. Later in life, she ran as the Farmer–Labor Party candidate for governor of the state of South Dakota and made a career for herself in public life, but, during my years at the academy, Alice Daly was a passionate and dedicated educator.

We had a study room at school that was intended to be a library; the shelves were in place, but there were no books. When Miss Daly discovered this lack, she immediately sent back east for her own collection. Later, when I got to Boston and Emerson College, I found my background in literature was as good as any of my classmates, all because of the influence and opportunities provided by this one teacher.

She also organized a kind of chautauqua, based on the adult education program popular then. She rented the local opera house and brought in play readers, male quartets, and lecturers—all of a very high standard. As there was no radio in those days, and few gramophones, these programs were the only opportunity we had to hear anything other than humdrum conversation about day-to-day concerns.

Miss Daly did all this on her own. She was a dynamo, an inspiration, and a catalyst for change in our community and in my life. When the time came for me to graduate from the academy, my mind was made up. I was going to Miss Daly's alma mater, Emerson College in Boston.

One beautiful day, my father presented me with a train ticket to Boston, with the strict injunction that I was not to lose it, to telegraph as soon as I reached Boston, and "don't talk to strangers." It was the fall of 1911, and I was almost nineteen.

I have never forgotten the excitement, the thrill of my first year in Boston. Emerson College was on Massachusetts Avenue, across the street from the great Boston Public Library, with its Edwin Abbey pictures of the Holy Grail, and Pierre Puvis de Chavannes murals, and the books, the books! There were the historic sites: Old North Church, Faneuil Hall, the Boston Common, and the Symphony Hall. The opera house and the art museum were built during my stay there.

The top balcony in Symphony Hall was open to patrons, mostly students, on Saturday afternoons for twenty-five cents. You had to stand in line with the exact coin ready to be dropped into a bag when the doors were opened. When so many bags were filled, that was it—the balcony was full and the doors were closed.

The first concert I attended there was, for me, a painful, chaotic experience. I had never before heard a lot of instruments playing together, except for the Pocatello Town Band tootling on Main and Centre streets on Saturday nights. At my first symphony concert, I could hear neither the instruments nor the melody—there were so many of them, and they all played at the same time. I couldn't tell when the orchestra stopped one piece and started another. The first symphony I ever really and truly heard was Beethoven's 5th, one grand and glorious Friday afternoon. It was as though a book had suddenly opened and I had just learned to read.

The courses at Emerson consisted of voice and speech training, body movement (i.e., gesture, based on the Dalcroze principles), interpretation, literature, and philosophy, largely rooted in the transcendentalism of Ralph Waldo Emerson. The courses in literature were particularly good, and there was also a course in Restoration drama. Looking back, I am amused to realize we never actually read the plays we studied—we just read about them, the period, and the authors. The professor probably thought the plays themselves were too salacious for us.

I graduated from Emerson in 1914 and, feeling well equipped, began to look for a teaching position. I quickly found that, with worries about war everywhere, few schools were hiring teachers for public speaking and oral expression. The First World War, when it started in August 1914, was considered strictly a European folly and was expected to last only a few months—"the boys will be out of the trenches by Christmas"—and, of course, we Americans would not be directly involved (or so we thought at the time).

Because of the war situation, my parents let me go back to Emerson to complete my postgraduate work. It was a very good thing I did, for once again Fate took a hand in shaping my future's course and destiny.

One day, my roommate came to me in great excitement. "Beany, you've got to do me a great favour. Please take me into Mrs. Black's class at eleven o'clock."

As an upperclassman, I was permitted to go into other people's classes to watch the teachers. But I was puzzled by my roommate's sudden enthusiasm for extra work. "Why on earth do you want to go?"

"Burton James is going to read Browning, and I simply *have* to hear him."

So we went to Mrs. Black's class at eleven. There, for the first time, I saw Burton James and heard him read Browning's "In a Gondola." He was talented, there was no doubt about it, with a magnificent voice and a sensitive understanding of his material. And he was definitely good-looking, not tall but slim and proudly erect, with a grace of carriage that always made him look elegant in anything he wore.

Sitting in that classroom, watching and listening, I knew exactly what I had to do. Shakespeare was right—Portia, Juliet, Helena, Viola, all had picked their men. I had picked mine. How far wrong can you go when Shakespeare gives direction? I set out on my new course of action with the same thorough concentration I had been applying to the acquiring of an education.

Each Sunday, my sorority sisters at the Zeta Phi Eta house held a tea. The young ladies' boyfriends came and brought their friends, so the young people could meet under properly chaperoned conditions. I had never held any interest in any of it.

The Sunday after the reading, I heard that one of my sorority sisters was bringing Burton James to tea. I rushed to get dressed. One of my sorority sisters popped into the room while I was getting ready and stared at me in amazement. "*You're* coming to the tea?"

I tried to be very nonchalant. "Yes, I thought I might just put in an appearance."

She looked at me narrowly. "I'll bet you're coming to meet Burton James." So much for my skills as an actress.

We met that Sunday, which was just around Christmas, and the rest of the winter was sheer bliss. We went to the Lowell lectures and heard Alfred Noyes and Robert Frost read their poetry. We heard Enrico Caruso in *Rigoletto* and saw Vaslav Nijinsky dance Debussy's *Afternoon of a Faun* and Sergei Diaghilev's production of *The Spectre of the Rose*.

Burton had come from a background far different from mine. His father, Frederick James, a farm boy from around Peekskill, New York, trained as a pharmacist and did very well in his profession, eventually operating a chain of twelve or fourteen drugstores in New York City and Brooklyn. Burton's mother came from a long line of Methodist ministers and bishops. They hadn't come over on the *Mayflower*, she admitted, but they had certainly arrived very shortly afterward. When Burton and I were living in New York and would go to the theatre with Mother James, she would survey the audience with distaste and remark, much too audibly, I always thought, "There are very few of us left."

With his mother's approval, and his father's accidental assistance, Burton became an avid theatregoer—Mr. James often received "comps" in return for the space he gave to playbills and posters in his stores and Burton made good use of them. Perhaps the most memorable was at Hammerstein's theatre—*A Night in an English Music Hall,* which included a young comedian with dark waves of hair surmounting a sensitive, plaintive face. He was listed on the program as Charles Chaplin.

At eighteen, Burton entered Cornell University for a five-year course in landscape architecture. In 1907, landscape architecture at Cornell had not settled into a defined area and it was unclear whether it was involved mainly with architecture or agriculture. Burton's courses included, besides architecture and architectural drawing, such varied and oddly assorted classes as cheese making, gasoline engines, agronomy, farm mechanics, and knot tying. However, Burton often said he had never learned anything—except possibly cheese making—that he could not profitably use for his own benefit and pleasure, and that of others.

His last job as a professional landscape architect was in 1913, with the widely known firm of Townsend and Fleming in Buffalo, New York, as Burton soon found another attraction in Buffalo that exerted a more powerful pull.

He began trying out for parts in the productions of the Studio Club. This was a time when great new things were beginning to happen in the theatre. Little theatre, community theatre, theatre for the people, theatre in out-of-the-way places, theatre for the actor, theatre for the scene designer with no actors (puppets only), theatre for the playwright—all of these theatres, generally very self-conscious and artistic, were pushing forward, putting down roots, and getting attention. They were usually held in great contempt by commercial theatre, but they persevered, survived, and were the forerunners of today's experimental and regional theatres.

Burton came to Emerson College to get the training he felt he needed to pursue his goal. He was an eager and enthusiastic student, the delight of teachers and classmates alike. He was imaginative and very skilful in constructing something interesting out of nothing. His brilliance—and his love—made my remaining months at Emerson joyous ones.

I graduated from my postgraduate course in May of 1915. After a summer working at a summer camp in Maine (during which I managed to spend a fair amount of time with Burton), we returned to Boston, Burton to finish his year at Emerson and I to a part-time teaching job at a convent school in the Boston suburbs. We began to make plans for a future for ourselves, together, in the theatre.

We were married on May 16, 1916, in Boston. His parents did not attend. My mother was to come east for the wedding, as Burton and I couldn't afford the trip to Pocatello, but my young brother was stricken with strep throat, so she didn't make it. My wedding, so far from my family, followed the precedent established by my mother so many years before. And I, too, had married a Protestant.

We agreed that our next step should be to New York, the big city, centre of all theatrical activity in the United States.

New York

In September 1916, I left for New York to try my luck with acting and see what the Fates might hold. Thousands before me had done it, and thousands are still doing it. Thousands undoubtedly had the same results I had, and perhaps came to the same conclusion—that it was not for me.

After making the rounds of the theatrical agents' offices, I wrote to Burton, still in Boston:

> I wish you could see the people lined up in these offices. I wish you could. They would make you shiver, such derelicts—awful! That's not what we want . . . The theatre is dreadful and these poor people looking for jobs in them—dreadful.
>
> Listen, today I read this sentence: "There is a time in every man's life and education

> when he arrives at the conviction that envy is ignorance, that imitation is suicide, that he must take himself for better or worse as his portion. Who would be a man must be a nonconformist."*

This letter was in a way prophetic, for it became for us a "habit of living." Burton never sat in an agent's office, having realized years earlier, while clerking in his father's drugstore, what I saw then in New York City's casting mills.

But we had to find some sort of work to keep us alive. Was there nothing, somewhere in New York, that we could do? Burton's sister Josephine was working as a secretary in the Lenox Hill Settlement House, then on East 69th and Avenue A. The settlements, as they were called, had grown out of an undertaking by Canon Barnett and his wife, who had set up similar institutions in a depressed area in London, England. They had seen the ignorance and the depression of the people of the neighbourhood and hoped to ameliorate it by providing education, a few cultural advantages, and a place where people could meet. The settlements were financed completely by donations from the well-to-do, who sat on committees or boards and directed the activities of the institution.

---

* Quoted from Ralph Waldo Emerson's essay "Self-Reliance."

I immediately saw them as a possibility for the use of our talents. I was so enthusiastic that I wrote to Burton immediately:

> This Lenox Hill Settlement is a perfect gold mine of opportunity for a neighborhood theatre. The people who come here are wonderful. The house is considered the very finest in the city in equipment. If you could only see what wealth is here.
>
> The house is heavily endowed, is loaded with equipment, and has absolutely nothing distinctly educational. Think what could be done if we could only get something to keep us alive, some work, perhaps our opportunity lies right here. The paid positions in the house are of course filled, but we could make a place for ourselves in a year.

So Burton joined me in New York, bringing with him all our worldly wealth: sixteen dollars and twenty-odd cents, all that was left after paying for his transportation out of the twenty-five dollars he had raised by pawning (on my instructions) the twin-diamond engagement ring that had been my mother's and was now mine.

The first job we got was for an agency organized by a man and his wife for the relief of the starving Albanians. They had printed up brochures with pictures of the miserable plight of the Albanian people and were asking for contributions. It was our job to stuff the brochures in envelopes and send them out. The husband was away, carting wheat to the Albanians, and management of the office had been left to the wife, who, unfortunately, was prone to temper tantrums, screaming, pulling her hair, frothing at the mouth. Burton and I would come out of the office at night so shaken we could scarcely eat.

When it seemed that both of us were bound to have nervous breakdowns, I found another job—as a file clerk and part-time switchboard operator in a brokerage office at 49 Wall Street. I'm sure I couldn't have realized what I was doing, taking a job as a Wall Street switchboard operator when the mechanics of operating a simple pencil sharpener threw me. I discovered that the frenzy of the woman at Albanian Relief was a spring breeze compared to what happens when the market starts going up or coming down. It was an experience, as I learned to say, that I shouldn't have picked and wouldn't have missed. I witnessed the lunacy of speculators first-hand, an education for anyone.

My salary was twelve dollars a week, and at Christmas they gave me a bonus of twenty-five dollars, a real kindness since I'd only been there for a few weeks. With this blessed yuletide windfall, I went merrily out and bought a wicker chair, some pots and pans, some extra sheets, and put the remainder of the money, twelve dollars, in a safe hiding place under the shelf paper in the kitchen cupboard of our tenement apartment. Unfortunately, in an excess of housewifely zeal while getting ready for the holidays, I cleaned the cupboards only a few days later and threw out the shelf paper, twelve dollars and all! Perhaps I knew even then that "easy come, easy go" on a field of empty pockets would be an appropriate heraldic emblem for the James family.

Our apartment was in a so-called model tenement in the Yorkville section, on 76th Street between Avenue A and John Jay Park. Our main, and largest, room was the kitchen, a comparatively spacious twelve by fifteen feet. There was, of course, no refrigeration (it hadn't been invented yet, or at least it hadn't reached 76th Street), but we did have a bathroom—a converted clothes closet.

The bedroom was larger than the bathroom, but smaller than the kitchen. In fact, when our friends at the settlement house kindly found us a bed, we discovered that the bedroom door couldn't be shut once the bed was moved in. Burton's drawing board, balanced on the radiator, was our dressing table, and that, along with an odd chair or two and a couple of pieces of carpet, completed the furnishing of our new home. Its main charm was the price—I believe it was three dollars a week, plus quarters for the gas meter. The cockroaches were a free bonus, and if there had been a bounty on them, we would soon have been rich.

Looking back on that particular period in our lives, it all sounds very grim and depressing, but I don't remember it being that way. We were young, healthy, optimistic, and very much in love. And we were sure we could cope with anything.

Well, just about anything. Though I was managing to keep up with the filing at my brokerage office, the switchboard was growing more and more malevolent. Even when it was quiet, it frightened me, but when it lit up like a Christmas tree, I was a quivering mass. I could see somebody's millions going down the drain because I'd pulled the wrong plug. So my chief emotion was one of overwhelming relief when I was finally fired. "Let go," I believe the euphemism is. And no captive was ever happier to be let go than I was.

Soon after that, we were having dinner at the settlement and a suffragette had been invited to be one of the guests. Votes for women had become an issue in England and the United States during the First World War, following not very quickly the introduction of the idea by John Stuart Mill in a speech at Westminster on March 30, 1867, in one of the early debates on the Reform Bill. Mill suggested that the time was ripe to give women the right to vote. The suggestion was greeted with loud guffaws from the British male, and *Punch* made good use of it in cartoons. British women—even the educated ones—quietly acquiesced to this male judgment of their inadequacies and incapacities, comforting themselves with the aphorism, "The hand that rocks the cradle rules the world." Then Emmeline Pankhurst and her daughters entered the scene.

As a student in Boston, I had heard Mrs. Pankhurst speak about women's problems in England. She was a gently spoken lady, dressed in a grey chiffon gown, carrying a bouquet of pink roses. She defended the extreme measures taken by the women of Britain in their struggle and said, "You American women can never understand the thick-headed, stubborn stupidity of the British male." Yet in 1917, all over the North American continent, women were rising, demanding the right to vote. It didn't seem a large or unreasonable request.

I had first recognized gaining the vote for women as an issue when I was attending Emerson, and it came as a surprise to me. Women in Idaho had had the vote for years. I can't ever remember my mother not going with my father to the polls to cast her ballot. Friends and relatives of both sexes and all ages frequently discussed politics in our home. But in Boston, for the first time, I heard women's suffrage described as if it would be a calamitous happening for women to get the vote, or even to become involved in the suffrage movement. Women would begin to frequent "grog shops," their children would land in the gutters, and home and motherhood would disappear.

I knew from my own experience this just wasn't so. My mother was not only a good mother and a good wife, she was a responsible citizen who cherished highly and took seriously her right and obligation to steer and shape our democratic nation.

My first real bit of political education had come from her, when I was about six years old. William McKinley had defeated William Jennings Bryan to become president of the United States. We, being westerners, had been for Bryan and against the famous "Cross of Gold."* In those days, the only "hot" news we ever got in Pocatello was from the trainmen, so it was from a trainman, calling to a neighbour, that I heard, "McKinley's been shot in Buffalo, New York!" I was delighted our "enemy" had been dispatched and ran to tell my mother.

To my amazement, Mother burst into tears. "But Mama, we didn't like him, did we?" She answered, through her tears, "Mr. McKinley is the president. We didn't want him for president, but the people elected him, and all the people have to support him. That's democracy."

Twenty years later, the lady at the settlement house dinner talked of the struggle women all across our democratic country were waging to win the right to vote. In the state of New York, they had to collect a million signatures to get suffrage on the ballot in the coming

* The Cross of Gold speech is remembered as one of the most famous in political history, and William Jennings Bryan advocated for a combined gold and silver standard to back America's currency, which thrust him into the Democratic nomination for president of the United States. It was a race he eventually lost to Republican William McKinley, and the United States formally adopted the gold standard in 1900.

election. They were looking for people to ring doorbells and talk to women and collect signatures.

She asked if I was interested. I certainly was, and when I heard they paid twelve dollars a week, which was what I'd been getting on Wall Street, I said yes right away and set out rapping on doors for the cause of women's suffrage. We got our million signatures and had a parade from 59th Street and Fifth Avenue to Washington Square. Many men marched with us in that parade, Burton among them. Suffrage was on the ballot and won. On November 6, 1917, the women of New York State got the right to vote.

Women today, in all parts of the country, are too often careless about exercising that right. They forget, if ever they knew, the struggle that was waged to get it. Women not only marched in parades and rapped on doors, they picketed the White House, they heckled speakers, they spoke from pulpits, they got themselves arrested, and at least one was killed. When they were thrown into jail, the suffragettes were generally put in the worst section, with the most hardened of the women prisoners. They made friends of these prisoners, and when the jailers in Washington discovered their charges weren't suffering enough, they opened a rat-infested jail that had not been in use since the Civil War and put them into that. The fact that many of these women were socialites from the first families made little difference. When they began demanding rights that the "establishment" of the day thought they did not need and should not ask for, masculine opinion was that they be taught a lesson. Mrs. Pankhurst had flattered the American male.

When the franchise was granted, the first presidential candidate we voted for, in 1920, was Eugene V. Debs, who was serving a term at the Atlanta Penitentiary for "obstructing" the First World War. He had said it was actually a power struggle for markets and that none of President Wilson's fourteen points, including the ideas that it was "the war to make the world safe for democracy" and "a war to end all wars," would ever be realized. The Treaty of Versailles had been signed, and we could discern the scaffolding that was to support the Second World War.

Through the summer of 1917, which was horribly hot in New York City—so hot that the Humane Society couldn't get around fast enough to pick up all the animals that dropped in the streets, and a dead horse lay on Park Avenue in the heat until it exploded—I was employed as a sort of social worker.

Mrs. James F. Curtis, a woman of wealth and good heart, had set up a project for those prostitutes, amateur and professional, who were picked up in raids on dance halls and bawdy houses and sent for treatment for venereal diseases to City Hospital. The "girls" ranged in age from twelve to seventy, and it was my job to supervise their training in how to run a sewing machine, bring them magazines, take them for walks, and try to prepare the way at home for their reception when they were released. Although I was twenty-four and married, I was still the quite-innocent product of a sheltered Catholic home, and it was a heart-wringing experience, a lot like trying to empty the ocean with a fork. The basic environmental situation could not be altered in any substantial way, the method was unorganized and unscientific, and the project never succeeded in becoming anything more than the goodwill gesture of a generous woman.

That fall I went to work, first for the state and then the Federal Food Board, as an inspector, at the unbelievably generous salary of one hundred dollars a month. (It took me from 1928 to 1946 to get my salary at the Playhouse up that high!) Since Burton had finally been put on staff at Lenox Hill as a playground and camp supervisor, at a salary of fifty dollars a month, we felt we were finally going to be able to make ends meet.

The Federal Food Board had been set up to control profiteering in food during the war. Every morning, food prices were listed in the paper. Grocers were supposed to sell food at the prices quoted, but of course in some instances they didn't. They also resorted to dubious practices, like forcing customers to buy a large order of groceries before they could get anything that was in short supply, such as sugar. Customers would send their complaints, enclosing their bills as proof, to the Federal Food Board, and inspectors would go out to investigate the complaints and later testify if charges were laid.

Three women and a couple of men actually did the work, but the staff also included a collection of terrible old crocks, political appointees who had been wangled into their jobs by some ward-heeler and spent most of their time sitting in the office playing cards. Our superior, a young and dedicated lawyer, depended on the five of us to get the work done. Sometimes he'd sigh, "I hate to send you women out on this complaint. It could be a rough one." He would then look around the office and say in a loud voice, tinged with resignation-blunted hope, "One of these men should do it." None of them ever did, at least not while I was there.

As a result of my war effort, I developed pneumonia and an ear infection, and was trundled off to New York's Roosevelt Hospital on 59th Street, five months pregnant, flaming with fever and in considerable pain because my ear had been operated on at the settlement house that afternoon.

I was a paying patient—fourteen dollars a week, I believe—but the only bed available to me was in the huge charity ward. I didn't care. I was too sick to worry about where I was. I only wanted to get better and to keep any part of my illness from affecting my baby. They had told me, quite casually, when I was admitted, that pneumonia in pregnancy was usually fatal to the woman or to her child—or both. I refused to think about that. "I've come this far," I said to myself. "I'm not going to give in now. I'm going to keep this baby."

Once a week, a doctor with a flock of students would gather round my bed and the doctor would expound about me and my case in the third person, explaining why this and that condition would make the patient's recovery highly unlikely, if not impossible. Then they would shake their heads sadly at the thought of me, so young, so pregnant, etc., etc., and pass on by. I thought to myself, as I lay there like some dummy on display, "You old dodo! I'll show you. I'm going to walk out of this place and take my unborn baby safely with me!"

The day came when doctor and students made their regular trek to my bedside to find me sitting up, hair neatly brushed, face set in a determined smile. The learned gentleman's jaw fell. "You're still here?" he sputtered. I laughed out loud at his amazement. "Still here. Alive. And getting well, I hope. *My* determination was better than your prognosis, Doctor. I had resources."

He harrumphed a bit then said, "I think I can discharge you today." I was out of there on wings. I had made up my mind that no child of mine would be born in a New York hospital. I had survived, but could a baby? So I went home to Pocatello, carefully, on the train, with a list of doctors and hospitals along the way, just in case. But my trip was uneventful, and our daughter, Mary Josephine or Marijo, was born on September 23, 1918.

The Settlement

Now that our baby had arrived safely, I was anxious to get back to New York, to Burton, and to work. But we expected Burton to be called in the draft at any time, he had not been able to find larger living quarters suitable for both a baby and us, and the dread influenza epidemic had struck New York.

As a settlement worker, Burton knew where the flu cases were in the Lenox Hill district, so he was riding the ambulances as a volunteer. He wrote that one trip had taken him out to a cemetery where he watched mass graves being dug with a steam shovel in order to accommodate the stacked and ticketed coffins that had piled up too fast to be handled in the usual fashion. After taking a hard look at the situation, Burton advised me to stay in Pocatello with Marijo for a while.

I did, but the flu soon struck there too. Just two weeks after I left the hospital, the "Spanish" influenza swept through it. Either the mother or the baby, and often both, of every maternity case there at the time died of the flu. As well, two of the Catholic Sisters of Mercy who had cared for the baby and me succumbed to the disease.

In the meantime, the war had ended in Europe. Burton would not be drafted. He was able to find us a place to live, an apartment in the two upper floors of a well-kept old brownstone at 318 East 69th Street, not far from Lenox Hill. We were to live there happily for three years.

A month to the day after the armistice, I left Pocatello with Marijo on a train that seemed to be crowded with servicemen. They took a great interest in the baby and helped us considerately on the long journey.

I was back home and ready to take up our struggle toward our eventual goals. Though our primary purpose in going into the settlement was to eventually build a theatre, we were forced to take a circuitous route. Miss Manning, the director, was interested in us and was trying to prepare a place for us on her staff. But it took time.

So at first we volunteered our services. I taught classes in "English for Foreigners." My classes consisted mostly of men who had applied for citizenship. There was no dignity or graciousness in these proceedings, but the men seemed grateful and I don't suppose the attitude was new to them. Given stories I'd heard from friends who worked as interpreters at Ellis Island, my students had probably experienced much the same treatment from their first moment after landing in "The Land of the Free."

Burton volunteered for work in the Lenox Hill gym and managed the Saturday night dances, for which there was a ten-cent admission charge. And we formed a drama group. Sports and the weekly dances attracted a great many young people to the settlement houses, but drama groups drew some of the more serious youngsters, and young people came from all over the city.

These young people, many of them American-born, growing up in slum neighbourhoods, going to overcrowded, unsanitary public schools, with the street corners and back alleys as playgrounds, were exposed to only the worst in American life, and many of them became real problems. Their charming, dignified, Old World parents would come to us at the settlement about their children's problems, and when we questioned them, they would say, "Our children pay no attention to us. They say we are greenhorns. This is America."

Burton and I hoped that perhaps a theatre at the settlement could bring some much-needed positive results. At first, our theatre work at the settlement was extracurricular. All lighting equipment, sets, and costumes had to be improvised, but we managed to produce many of the one-act plays of J.M. Barrie and George Bernard Shaw, one or two original plays, some pantomime, Ibsen's *An Enemy of the People*, and Shakespeare's *Twelfth Night*.

As there were always more women than men in the drama group, the job of directing fell to me. It was exhausting, often frustrating, and frequently rewarding, especially when some progress could be made or some spark of talent fanned. One such spark was in a young Irish lad, just past his middle teens, stockily built, with a boxer's shoulders and dancer's legs, and the typically Hibernian red hair, blue eyes, and lavish freckles. His father was a bartender in Yorkville, his mother a wonderfully indomitable woman whose spirit seemed more than a match for poverty. The boy was one of a clamouring and nonconforming clan of four brothers and one sister who shared the honest Irish patronymic of Cagney. His name was James . . . Jimmy.

Jimmy's brother Harry, later a physician in New York, arrived at Lenox Hill first and soon brought his brother along. Jimmy did his first acting under our direction and attacked it with the earnest dedication with which he tackled everything. From time to time he would disappear from our acting group, and then we would know he was working. Mrs. Cagney was dogged and inventive in her desperate determination to see that her brood got an education. The little girl, Jeanne, was still a baby, but the four boys had to have schooling. So they would take turns: two would go to school while the other two worked. Then, after a time, they would trade places.

Jimmy was a fine and dedicated performer, and also a handy fellow to have around the theatre in other capacities as well. The hard-fisted physical prowess he so often displayed in his movies was never a mere cinematic invention. As a kid in Yorkville, you had to know how to take care of yourself, particularly if you cared much about living long enough to grow up.

One May night, in 1921, we were doing a performance of Ibsen's *An Enemy of the People*. Some neighbourhood rowdies who didn't go for this "art" stuff began throwing rocks through the gym-auditorium windows and started to make an organized sortie into the building's backstage and dressing rooms by way of the fire escape. Jimmy wasn't in the cast, but he was around, and when Burton, dressed for the character of Morten Kiil, started after the intruders with his cane, Jimmy appeared, whispering hoarsely, "It's all right, Mr. James. Go back to your acting. We'll take care of them."

For the next few moments, Henrik Ibsen's excoriation of private and municipal corruption was performed against an unrehearsed counterpoint of muffled cries that drifted in from the alley. *Smack!* "Ow!" *Smack! Smack!* "Aw right! We'll pay!" *Smack!* "We'll pay! We'll pay!" And pay they did, with coin as well as with blood, black eyes, and tears.

Jimmy's elegant muscular equipment served him well in less warlike pursuits as well. He was a first-rate ball player and an excellent boxer. He was interested in drawing. But most of all, he was a dancer and when, toward the end of our stay in New York, he decided to take the plunge and go into show business, he became first a chorus boy and then a "hoofer." He used to bring his partner, a pretty little girl named Billie, back to the settlement for a place to rehearse their dance routines. We weren't surprised when they got married soon after, or when Jimmy's career went steadily uphill to the very top of the entertainment field.

It was for all the young people like Jimmy that we persisted in our dream of providing theatre that would open doors and bridge chasms. As well as artistic considerations, our early plays grew out of social necessity. We did plays at Lenox Hill to help centre the interests of disintegrating families on things they had in common. Our work grew out of trying to preserve family units that were falling apart in the New World. We urged the Czechs and Hungarians and Italians to put on festivals and pageants representative of their homelands, to conserve the art they had brought with them to America. They were being laughed at and looked down upon, and their children needed exposure to something they could take pride in, both in their past as well as something better in their future.

Finally, Miss Manning and her board of trustees began to look with approval on the work of our drama group. Burton, who had been put on staff full-time at a salary of $125 a month, was given an extra $100 a month for the theatre work he was doing in the evenings and on weekends. In effect, the board received "two for the price of one," as my work with the Lenox Hill Players remained on a volunteer basis for as long as we were there. However, in February of 1919, I finally achieved my goal of joining the staff at Lenox Hill—though certainly not in any way I might have imagined.

Lenox Hill Settlement House was situated in a Polish, German, Hungarian, Czech, and Italian neighbourhood. The men in many of these families were highly skilled workers, craftsmen in factories making surgical instruments or pianos, or employed as cigar makers. Their salaries were not lavish, but they were adequate in most cases, and they were generally steady. Then the First World War intervened. Drafted men were paid only thirty dollars a month, so families whose breadwinners had been called to fight for Uncle Sam faced hardships. Many of the women who had been left to eke out a living for their families were skilled embroiderers, and it occurred to someone that their peasant embroidery might find a market. So the Mothers' Club of the settlement, composed mostly of Czechoslovakian women, organized a sort of cottage industry for the manufacture and sale of this colourful needlework.

I was working with the Mothers' Club as a volunteer at the time and the embroidery project interested me. I watched, asked questions, and trotted down to the library to read all I could about this art/craft and the Moravian communities in which it originated. The infant project caught on. It was the beginning of the popularity of "peasant" fashion decoration, which has waxed and waned but never entirely disappeared. The ladies decided the project should be expanded and to that end sent me on behalf of the Mothers' Club to the Lenox Hill Board of Trustees to request a modest amount of money so a designer and trained salesperson could be hired. To my surprise, and delight, the board not only voted for the money for the project but hired me on the spot to head it up.

At first, I was laughed at when I tried to interest dress designers and garment manufacturers in our output. "No American woman would ever wear that stuff," they said, although I was wearing it and I liked it. Gradually, however, we gained a market, though it never reached the proportions it would achieve in later years. Our efforts, however, led to an even more important development.

The committee meeting of the Lenox Hill Board of Directors was attended by Mrs. Marshall Field, wife of the Chicago millionaire. She was building a home, which she was furnishing with fabulous antiques imported from abroad. The furniture came into the country duty-free, because it was more than a hundred years old, but the duty on imported coverings to reupholster it came to nearly 100 percent. At the meeting, Mrs. Field said, "I am not interested in peasant embroidery, but if you can do crewel embroidery to recreate the traditional materials I need, I will loan you six thousand dollars to get started." She turned to me. "Do you think you can do it?"

I had never heard of crewel embroidery, but I said, "I think we could try." As soon as we left the meeting, I rushed to the library to find out what kind of embroidery could be "crewel"—at that point, I didn't even know how to spell it. I found it is one of the most ancient forms of embroidery, dating back to the fifth century in Egypt, and takes its name from the use of a special "crewel" yarn, a fine wool yarn with a slight sheen that usually comes in two plies twisted into a single strand. Crewel work is durable, perfect for household and personal accessories.

When we began our new project, we were really starting from scratch—we had to import the wools, the backgrounds, and just about everything we needed. I hired a skilled embroideress who taught the less skilled, stitch by stitch, and I haunted the museums, using a magnifying glass to study the fabrics, yarns, and stitches of centuries-old originals.

Burton, along with his duties in the drama group and supervising the gym and the dances, became our designer. As soon as the project became known, we began to get orders from decorators all over the city. The whole scheme was a great success. The women were gainfully employed and delighted to use their skills in this new effort, and I became knowledgeable enough in the craft to keep things going.

Thinking back, I am sure that one of the reasons I, in particular, was able to do so much at that time was that

Marijo turned out to be an extremely accommodating and self-sufficient baby. I would rise early (a habit I've never been able to break), breastfeed our daughter, then get dressed and make breakfast. That done, I'd walk the block and a half to the settlement to get the day's work started in the embroidery shop.

After an hour or so, I'd go back to the apartment, bathe Marijo, give her a 10:00 a.m. feeding, open the windows, wrap her up, put her down for her nap, and go back to work. I usually ate lunch at the settlement, but at 2:00 in the afternoon I'd go home again to give the baby hers. The rest of the day was spent in the shop, which closed at 4:30 so I could be back home in time to feed Marijo again and put her to bed. Between my visits, she was left to her own devices, at first in her crib and later in a playpen. The people in the apartment downstairs were there, of course, and looked in on her from time to time, but really she was on her own.

Always, though, Marijo was a part of us and what we were doing. At night, I'd take her to rehearsals, and she'd sleep or wake up and play around, never causing a fuss, never getting in the way. Back then our methods of child-rearing seemed natural. I don't think I'd do it that way now.

One of the side benefits of the embroidery project was that Burton and I came in contact with the ethnic groups in the neighbourhood and their interest in music, dance, and even opera. These new Americans produced plays they had known in the countries from which they'd emigrated. The ethnic groups welcomed our suggestion that perhaps something could be done to provide more adequate surroundings for this type of activity. Burton proposed a folk theatre, and we approached the settlement director, Miss Manning, with the idea. She was most enthusiastic. She, too, wanted the settlement to become an enlarged centre for cultural activities and took the matter up with her board. There was a vacant lot next to the settlement house, which seemed ideal for expansion. The board agreed, and Burton designed his first theatre, a forty-thousand-dollar structure, and came up with ways and means of financing it.

I am sure that many members of the board recognized our idea as a positive step in the process of Americanization for our neighbourhood's minorities. We made our plans, hoped, prepared, and waited. From time to time, some encouraging things did happen.

But though the people of the community, the staff of the settlement house, and Burton and I were enthused and ready to get to work, there seemed to be no particular haste on the part of the Lenox Hill board to proceed with things. When we submitted our plan for the final approval of the full board, it was tabled and another proposal was brought forward—forty thousand dollars would enlarge the gym and build a swimming pool. The recession of 1922, a mere preamble to the crash of 1929, had frightened possible investors in culture and

Americanization. A tennis court eventually sprouted on the site Burton had selected for a folk theatre, and we began to feel that perhaps the board-dominated settlement house milieu was destined to remain fallow ground as far as our dreams for a people's theatre were concerned.

A New, Fresh Wind

We were more than a little downhearted as we left that summer for jobs at the children's camp in Maine. Then we received a telegram from Nellie Cornish of the Cornish School in Seattle, Washington, offering us positions on her staff. If we accepted, it would mean giving up the advantages of the big city—which were greater then, I think, than now. We had put down roots at Lenox Hill. We liked much of the work we were doing there, and we loved the people in the neighbourhood where we lived.

We decided I should go to New York for the interview while Burton would remain in Maine to finish the work we were doing there. When I met Miss Cornish in New York, I was somewhat surprised by her appearance. She was short in stature and inclined to corpulence, and in no way resembled a dreamer of dreams or the director of an art school.

We liked each other immediately, but she was disappointed that Burton had not come with me. As she told me, with her characteristic forthrightness, she was more interested in him than in me. She had already engaged someone to direct plays and teach the acting courses. What she really needed now was a person to teach stage design, stage construction, and lighting, and to act as a producer. There was an opening for me if I could teach speech and "elocution."

My education at Emerson had given me the skills to do this work, although I took a very dim view of its value. I could see little point in teaching young people to "speak pieces" for the gratification of their parents and the boredom of everyone else who had to listen to them. I believed speech presented special problems and needed special instruction.

When Burton finally arrived in New York for his interview, Miss Cornish was pleased with him, as well she should have been. He was personable, talented, energetic, ambitious, and had the techniques and skills to teach the backstage work she needed in her theatre department. She offered us contracts, which we accepted, and we prepared to pull up our stakes in New York and go west. I was to go immediately to prepare classes in my adaptation of the disputed elocution, and to find living quarters for Burton, myself, and four-year-old Marijo.

It was raining the morning I arrived in Seattle. The porter who helped me off the train at first expressed concern I had neither raincoat nor umbrella. Then he reassured me that it really didn't matter, as "Seattle rain doesn't get you wet."

Seattle is a beautiful small city, with the Olympic and Cascade mountain ranges, Puget Sound, and the lakes. A new, fresh wind seemed to be blowing. Energy and imagination were in the air.

Something must be said here about the state of Washington, which was probably the last of the frontiers of the continental United States to be settled, as what we were able to accomplish there was, to a great extent, influenced by the history and development of the state and its people. In the 1880s and 1890s, hordes of the dispossessed from the eastern United States and Europe crossed the continent to Washington, fleeing railroad blacklists, wheat famines, and the wage slavery of the mines and mills to seek freedom and security in this faraway corner of the country. Many came in groups, bought land, and established colonies where they could freely profess their beliefs in cooperation, religion, or socialism. The dedication, energy, and struggles of these colonists to hold on to their beliefs now seem incredible. Many thought if they could establish the sort of society Eugene Debs described, one that could "dethrone Gold and elevate humanity," in one corner of this vast country, the rest of it would follow and "transform the days to come into a virtual paradise."* Those whom the colonists saw as their oppressors also thought this might be a possibility and feared it.

In the years that followed, many of the hopeful migrants failed to find the paradise they had come for and became instead migratory labourers in the forests, in the mills, and on the docks. Their frustrations eventually drove them to organize a militant union called the Industrial Workers of the World, thoroughly hated by lumber and waterfront employers. The stage for battle, sometimes bloody, always bitter, was set.

Reading today of the violence and vehemence of these struggles, the simplicity of the causes is amazing: unionism, the eight-hour day, free speech, an uncensored press, freedom from poverty in old age, and unemployment and health programs. And for many of them, accepted in principle but not in practice, the struggle is far from over.

I was enchanted with my first glimpse of the Cornish School. It was situated on the corner of a tree-lined street in a residential area. The architecture was something called Spanish baroque, different from anything else in the city, and was covered with peach-coloured stucco, trimmed in sage green, with touches of dogwood as the decorative motif. It was unmistakably a school of the arts.

---

* Quoted from a letter written by Eugene Debs to John D. Rockefeller, June 19, 1897.

Miss Cornish wanted only the best instructors for her school, and she had a genius for attracting such people. Eminent artists, when they visited the school and saw its program and activities, frequently returned as members of the faculty to teach summer school and sometimes became permanent members of the staff. Among these were Adolph Bolm, formerly of Diaghilev's Ballets Russes and later ballet master for the Chicago Civic Opera; Myron Jacobson, a graduate of the Petrograd Imperial Conservatory and, after he fled the Russian Revolution, accompanist for Feodor Chaliapin; and many others of equal distinction. The yet-unrecognized Mark Tobey taught painting. And Martha Graham said Miss Cornish permitted her, as an unknown, to give a performance one Sunday evening "on pure speculation."

Dancer Merce Cunningham and composer John Cage were students at the school. One Sunday evening, Cage was to give a lecture-recital on modern music. He was not much of a lecturer and said so, adding, "I think I'd better show you." He ran his hands over the piano keys, sometimes using his fists and elbows, then ran around the piano and played the strings. His lecture and his performance were equally mystifying to the audience.

It was an exciting, challenging place to be. Burton arrived with Marijo and we set to work enthusiastically to build a life for ourselves in this dynamic environment.

Burton was to teach stage design and technical skills, and he began in his tactful but effective way to mould his classes and courses into shape. I had problems in the speech department due to the existing tradition of "florid" elocution. I still remember one of my first students rendering Vachel Lindsay's "The Congo" while hammering on a table with two sticks. Another typical "piece" was presented by a young girl who had selected a hundred lines from Shakespeare for recitation. She had picked the hundred lines she thought were "most beautiful" and mixed them into a literary hash that even Shakespeare himself would probably not have recognized.

However, we knew what we wanted to achieve and slowly but steadily worked toward it with rewarding results. I taught the acting course and directed the plays, and Burton continued his classes in stage design and construction. We received a combined salary of $400 a month, which would rise to $440 after about two years.

In our third year at the school, Burton suggested a series of programs by the music, dance, drama, and opera departments for the coming 1926–27 season. It would serve as a "showcase" for the school and contribute to Seattle's cultural life. And subscription sales of tickets could be created to provide money for production costs. The plan was accepted and there were enthusiastic audiences in full houses.

In the 1927–28 season, however, the other departments began to feel pressured by the deadlines involved. As Burton had initiated the whole showcase idea, the

Drama Department was blamed for the pressure, and the claim was made that the school was becoming "too professional." Fortunately, as the schedule had been set and tickets sold, we managed to get through the year's program.

In August of 1927, Burton was engaged as technical director by the Wayfarer Pageant Society to stage a mammoth production of Giuseppe Verdi's *Aida* at the University of Washington Stadium. Five prominent singers from the Metropolitan Opera in New York City—Frances Peralta, Marion Telva, Paul Althouse, Fred Patton, and William Gustafson—were imported to perform the leading roles under Karl Krueger's direction. The production was not connected with the school, but a number of the faculty and students were involved. The production was tremendously successful and even nature gave an added fillip to the stage effects—on opening night, the moon rose behind the set, as if on cue, to a round of admiring applause.

We felt our success in such activities, as well as the appreciation of our productions at Cornish, which frequently played to standing-room-only audiences, redounded to the credit of the school. We began to see, however, that there were some who feared Burton might expand beyond the orbit of the little school and resented it.

The situation at Cornish was frustrating, so in November of 1927, I took a trip back east to see what was going on in the "real" theatrical world. I visited the Cleveland Play House, the Kenneth Sawyer Goodman Memorial Theatre in Chicago, the Eastman School of Music's Drama Department, the Civic Repertory Theatre in Boston, and Professor George Pierce Baker's new school of theatre at Yale. Then I spent three weeks in New York, seeing a total of thirty-three plays, mostly bad.

When I returned, thankfully, to Seattle, I gave lectures on the debility and sterility of American drama. I spoke at teas, women's clubs, and drama leagues and was interviewed by the press. My rejection of what I had seen went much deeper than a superficial scoffing at commercialism: "Our whole theatrical stream has been frozen by our Puritan ancestor, and it will probably take a thousand years to thaw it out." When I said that, I had no idea that very soon that same puritanism would rear its head to breathe frostily over our own shoulders.

We were in dress rehearsal for Luigi Pirandello's *Six Characters in Search of an Author*, when Miss Cornish called us to her office. Some member of the board had heard (though Miss Cornish admitted none of the board members had actually read the play) that *Six Characters* was immoral and would do the school inestimable damage if produced on the Cornish stage. It must be withdrawn at once. The board then issued an edict that all future Cornish plays must be submitted to it for prior approval. This directive would have created an untenable situation for any artistic director. The director alone must be responsible for play choice, as only he or she knows the casting and staging problems and what is planned for the material.

The only reason given for the dictum was the arbitrary one of immorality, which we found hard to accept, as did the students working on the production and anyone to whom we spoke who had actually read the script. The most likely motive for killing the play seemed to be the unspoken but tacit fear that we were trying to turn the Cornish School into a theatre. There were fervent protests from the students and faculty over the board's censorship, but for the first and only time in our lives, we cancelled a date and produced something else to fill the commitment.

Six Characters was not withdrawn without a struggle, and some of the cordial relations we had previously enjoyed went with it. In various ways, we were made to feel that "School was School" and that perhaps our aspirations were too ambitious. Finally, in the spring of 1928, we decided to resign and establish a theatre that would be free to do the adult and professional things we were most interested in. So we left, with some of the more mature young people who had been our students and co-workers. We hoped to become co-workers in the establishment of a living theatre.

Our years at Cornish were happy, fruitful ones, in spite of internal politics and the usual frustrations and frictions involved in any job. The people we met at the school, either as students or teachers, remained fast friends and gave us lasting memories of a happy, stimulating association.

Tenuous Rocks

On a Sunday afternoon in May 1928, a few days after our departure from the Cornish School, a group of friends gathered in our apartment to talk about establishing a theatre. We all agreed that Seattle needed a noncommercial theatre where artists could work as a group, refining their skills and accumulating experience so they could become a competent acting and producing company. We wanted a theatre in which community involvement was central, so that any defeat or triumph for the theatre would be one for the community as well. We planned to uncover and awaken the common bond of creative responsibility that welds the artist to the people.

Most of the people in the group were no longer students in the school sense but adults, entering that greater classroom, the world, where the questions posed are not hypothetical but all-important ones that challenge and possibly change the whole flow of lives. Could they earn a living? What about getting married, having children, acquiring a home and security? Would they be able to "make it," or would they become artistic drifters, always pursuing phantom careers and always on the fringe of poverty? Could they meet the future?

The questions applied to Burton and myself as well, of course. We had had a fairly strong taste of reality already. We had a daughter. We had responsibilities. But we also had faith, and a dream, and on those tenuous rocks we were determined to build our future.

We were confident our theatre could succeed, because it would rise *from* the community, rather than being imposed *on* it from outside. Seattle was our community. Our theatre would belong to our community and would become the possession of every neighbour who entered its doors. The theatre and the community would become inseparable members of the same social family. It was the only way to triumph over the commercial competition of movies and road shows. And it was the only way in which we, as artists, could survive under a system of industrialized culture.

Burton and I scoured the city of Seattle looking for some building or part of a building that would serve our purposes—lofts, old churches, lodge halls, stables; we looked at anything and everything that could conceivably be converted into a theatre. We finally rented a vacant hole-in-the-wall building on University Way to serve while we continued looking. We bought a few furnishings—table, desk, chairs—for, as I remember, twenty-seven dollars, installed a telephone, and began a promotional campaign for our plays, which would open in October.

An anonymous donor sent us an unsolicited cheque for five hundred dollars to get the campaign going. The angels smiled. We were operating on a season ticket basis, six plays for five dollars, which would give us our working capital. The theatre-going public knew us from our work at Cornish and that first season we sold 997 tickets before a single play had been produced.

Burton was firmly convinced the theatre should be self-sustaining and felt subsidies limit freedom of operation. Today, I suppose this would be considered quixotic, as it is generally recognized that all performing art must be subsidized in order to exist.

Though we had had experiences at Lenox Hill and Cornish that made us leery of boards and board dictatorship, we still felt our theatre needed a board to provide backing, prestige, a socially stabilizing force, and a link to our community. We intended to limit the board's powers when it came to such things as play choice and casting, and we did not want a board committed to personal financial support for the theatre, an arrangement we were certain would become ingrown and constricting, both socially and artistically.

Our first board was composed of some of Seattle's first citizens, well-known men and women who came together to act as sponsors and advisors, lending their names for prestige only. One of these was Glenn Hughes, head of the University of Washington's School of Drama.

Many of our friends, solicitous of our future and that of our theatre, suggested Seattle might not be the best place to start. Why not Portland, or San Francisco? There was a curious humility in the city about its place in culture and the arts. People thought artists who chose to come to, or to stay in, Seattle could not be very good—if they were, they would be in New York or San Francisco or anywhere else.

To excite interest in our new undertaking, and to promote sales of our season tickets, we publicized the program the theatre would undertake: a children's play series, a one-act play contest, dance programs, opera *intime*, productions of plays by local authors, a state-wide play festival, and tours of successful productions. Eventually, most of this program came to fruition.

We filed articles of incorporation that set the theatre up as a nonprofit corporation, without stockholders and with surpluses, if any, to be ploughed back into the institution. I may say that the problem of surpluses never caused us much trouble. Anyone excited about "free enterprise" should have worked with us over the years. We were as enterprising as all get out, and as free as the birds to go hungry if necessary. No one was getting a salary, though expense money for food and a roof was provided when necessary. We never had financial incentives, tax relief, or subsidies, but we managed somehow. (At one time, we were paying five different taxes and the Washington State Legislature, when it amended its tax bill, included "repertory theatre" by name, so we could not escape.)

Everything seemed to be going well. We were working toward the opening of our first season, rehearsing Seán O'Casey's *Juno and the Paycock* and Ferenc Molnár's *The Guardsman*, building scenery, making costumes, and wondering where in the world we could play the shows. As time was getting short and the dates were set, we finally settled on the Metropolitan Theatre in downtown Seattle. It had an enormous overhead for our limited resources, but there were some advantages: it was Seattle's most highly regarded road show theatre, and the public would associate us with all the professional troupes that had played there. We felt we needed to impress on the average theatregoer that we were no longer a student group but a company of theatre artists.

We had announced that our first plays would be *The Guardsman*, *Juno and the Paycock*, and Sem Benelli's *The Jest*. The first was a comedy, the second a realistic tragedy, and the third a pageant-like melodrama. All three had been recent Broadway successes and had never been seen in Seattle.

Ten days before our announced opening, the Theatre Guild wired that *The Guardsman* was not available for Seattle. Publicity, sets, costumes, and rehearsals all had to be scrapped at the eleventh hour, and *Juno and the Paycock* (which luckily had been in rehearsal at the same time) was moved up to fill the number-one spot.

We had not wanted to open with such a starkly realistic tragedy, but there was no alternative. *Juno and the Paycock* is a great play—one of the greatest. It is also the sort of play some playgoers label "depressing," so it made a difficult pacesetter for our first season. But it was a great thrill for all of us when O'Casey sent a handwritten letter giving us permission to produce the play in Seattle at five pounds a performance.

The Seattle Repertory Playhouse launched in October 1928 with four performances of *Juno*. We played to fair audiences and had good reviews. Our total costs for the production came to $1,200. We earned $1,100. On the surface, it looked as though we had lost only $100, but that didn't take into account such things as office rental, sales costs, staff expenses (minimal though they were), publicity, and general overhead.

The Jest, a melodrama laid in Renaissance Italy, presents a number of technical problems to a successful production and we hoped to use it to establish the technical competence of our young company. We needed eighteen-foot sets for the production. Hugo Alde, our stage technician, told us he knew of some flats, stored in an old warehouse, that could be purchased cheaply. We went to have a look at them and found they were covered in linen. Mr. Alde told us that linen had been used as ballast on Russian ships coming to Seattle ports, then dumped on the docks when cargo was loaded and could be taken away for little or nothing. We purchased the flats for around four hundred dollars.

Catherine Stetsky, who had been a costumier in pre-revolutionary Russia and had worked for us at Cornish, was turned loose among bolts of silk, brocades, taffetas, bundles of fur, and hanks of lace to create an eye-filling display of stage dresses and uniforms. An elegant spectacle was in the making, a calculated investment in our future.

Both audiences and critics praised the play for the skill, beauty, and lavishness with which it was presented. We had acquired a good deal of material that could be (and was!) used over and over, and our theatre's reputation for production was indelibly etched in the public's mind. We had spent more than five hundred dollars on scenery, four hundred dollars on costumes, nearly six hundred dollars on advertising, plus properties, royalties, rental for the Metropolitan Theatre, and the cost of hiring some stagehands. The total cost of mounting the production, fantastic as it seems now, considering the costs of plays today, came to nearly three thousand dollars. We took in less than half that amount.

When we were informed that our first four months of operation had cost over one thousand dollars a month, we realized some drastic curtailment was necessary. The Metropolitan Theatre was definitely out; other arrangements had to be made and we finally rented the auditorium at the Women's Century Club. The auditorium was attractive, with seating capacity for between 350 and 400, and we occupied it for the rest of that playing season and for our second year. We also decided to eliminate all paid advertising and to rely on the free space provided by local newspapers for our press releases. And no salaries, whatsoever.

We wound up our first year in operation with an income of $9,771.60, and expenditures of $11,129.73—a deficit of $1,358.13. But we had gained invaluable stature in the esteem of our audiences and potential audiences, had stockpiled a good deal of material for reuse, and had begun to achieve the things we had set out to do—the production of original plays by local playwrights, for example.

We had also begun to develop the wonderful camaraderie that was one of the strongest pillars of the Playhouse throughout its existence. One of the events that contributed to this was our first Christmas dinner on stage. Only the cast and crew of the current Christmas play attended that first dinner, but it became an annual Playhouse event, frequently attended by as many as 150 guests, with special invitations going to the members of our board, the mayor, and other local or visiting notables.

Our second season, 1929–30, opened with Molnár's *The Guardsman,* followed by an original script, *The Chaste Mistress* by Marianne King, a young playwright from

San Francisco. Louisa M. Alcott's *Little Women* was our Christmas production. We also toured to Everett, Washington, playing *The Guardsman*, Ibsen's *The Master Builder*, and Gregorio Martínez Sierra's *The Romantic Young Lady*. Another original script was *L'Envoi* by Albert M. Ottenheimer, now an actor with our group. We concluded the season with Luigi Pirandello's *Six Characters in Search of an Author*, the play that had seemed so controversial at the Cornish School. It now played without adverse comment or censorship of any kind.

In two years of operation, we had produced twelve plays for subscription audiences, three of which were original scripts. Two plays, not included in subscriptions, were for young audiences. And we had gone on tour—to one city, it was true, but it was a beginning. And we finished our second season without a staggering deficit, something unheard of in the annals of regional theatres.

While we were playing at the Women's Century Club, we realized that as long as we were in rented quarters, our development and expansion, both artistically and financially, would be held back. For instance, without control over our playing space, it was impossible for us to extend runs. We had to have a home of our own. After our fruitless search for premises, we decided to build, preferably in the university district, with its convenient location.

I remember vividly the day Burton came into our little office and said, "I've been looking at that old building on the corner of 41st and University Way. With the vacant lot that's right next to it, it might really make a fine theatre." He called Arthur Loveless, one of Seattle's leading architects, and they went up the street to look at the property. Mr. Loveless saw possibilities in the location. They went to a restaurant for coffee and sketched out the plans on paper napkins. Their plans remained unaltered in the final building.

We approached banks for loans and were told that what we wanted was money for a "specialty" building and that that kind of money was difficult, almost impossible, to borrow. We were somewhat less daunted when we were informed that hospitals, churches, country clubs, libraries, and many others were "specialty" buildings.

Our accountant said, "I know a man who specializes in specialty buildings." Specialist Wendell Pike seemed not at all perplexed by the problem and within what seemed a remarkably short time obtained the loan from the Prudential Savings and Loan Company. A ninety-nine-year lease was drawn up and duly executed around these plans, with a multitude of legal stipulations attached to the venture.

When I reread the complicated arrangements and think of the rabbit-like costs that multiplied seemingly overnight, I am appalled at our temerity. We did all this with the consent and approval of our board of directors, who were good businessmen. But none of us realized that not prosperity but the worst depression the United States or the world had known was just around the corner.

With the major financing accomplished, we had to find money for installations and the various other unexpected and surprising expenses that came up as the building progressed. Once, Burton and Al Ottenheimer went up and down the avenue to raise eleven hundred dollars that was urgently required to keep the contractor happy and the bricklayers laying bricks. They sold life memberships for one hundred dollars apiece and debenture notes of fifty or one hundred dollars. By the end of the afternoon, they had raised the needed funds. This was what our board called "junior financing."

With a good deal of help from our friends, and what seemed like endless hours of toil, the Repertory Playhouse gradually took shape. Our theatre, just as Arthur Loveless and Burton had sketched it on restaurant napkins, became a reality. It opened on October 30, 1930, the third season of the Seattle Repertory Playhouse.

Major Barbara, our opening play, went well in spite of problems getting it on. The reviews were good, tickets were selling, and we were optimistic. We knew where we had come from and where we were going. We had a home of our own, although bewildering challenges lay ahead.

We had produced Seán O'Casey, Henrik Ibsen, and George Bernard Shaw in the same season. As one columnist observed, "John Public has right-about-faced. You see him standing in line to buy tickets to Shaw, Ibsen, and Shakespeare, and you see him coming out after the performance with that certainly-got-my-money's-worth expression." We did not do slight comedies to attract the unsophisticated theatregoer, as most new producers think they must. Great drama attracted audiences, and they paid their way.

The second play in our third season was another original script, *Leading Man*, a satiric comedy on Hollywood by William Kimball. *Billboard* carried a review of the play with a picture of the Playhouse and commented on the importance the production of new playwrights by theatres such as ours had on the development of theatre, plays, and playwrights for the country at large.

In the spring of 1930, we made a decision that was to have a significant impact on our theatre and its development. Since our student days, we had been interested in Ibsen's *Peer Gynt*. Most actors dream of plays and parts they would *like* to play, and my husband, I am sure, had for a very long time dreamed of the day when he would play Peer. It was a fascinating play, a challenging play, a prestigious play, a good play. So we decided that one of the first productions in our new theatre would be *Peer Gynt*. Our board of directors was understandably concerned about such a production, with its large cast, an orchestra to play Edvard Grieg's music, and an abundance of production costs. I suppose it didn't seem like the wisest choice, faced as we were at the time with mountains of bills. But, as publicist and playwright Al Ottenheimer later described it, "Starry-eyed with the idealism which characterized some of our decisions, as frequently wrong as right, we went ahead."

The Shadow of Victory

Our production of *Peer Gynt* was to be the fifth presentation of the play in the United States. Henrik Ibsen had written the play as a poem in five acts and thirty-eight scenes. It is said that once, as a birthday celebration, the total play was produced in two evening performances and Ibsen fell asleep in the middle of it! We obviously had to adapt it, so we arranged it in three parts and fifteen scenes. Ibsen himself had said, "Of course it's impossible to stage *Peer* except in an abbreviated form. I shall be satisfied as long as the piece is reduced to a proper length. Not to do this would spoil everything."

The first announcement of the production of the play was in the *Town Crier* in September 1930. For weeks, the press publicized the proposed production of *Peer Gynt* by a local group. "The theatrical event of the decade in Seattle," wrote the *Jewish Transcript*. "It will be, in every respect, a production unparalleled in the dramatic annals of Seattle," said the *Seattle Times*. To give the public a better understanding of the play's position as literature and drama, we arranged for a series of lectures for our subscribing members with professors from the university, discussing Ibsen's masterpiece on Sunday afternoons preceding the opening. This proved to be a wise move, for the subsequent long run was no doubt partly due to this scholarly popularization of the piece.

The cast of sixty included those in sectors of the cultural life of Seattle that had never before been engaged in a cooperative effort of this magnitude. The city's Scandinavian community entered enthusiastically into our preparations. One man called to ask if I would like him to paint the barn as Norwegians would have painted it!

The production, in playing time alone, took three hours, so long scene changes were obviously out. Robert Mahaffy designed a set that was ultramodern in approach and execution, allowing the entire drama to be played on a series of levels against a seemingly limitless expanse of blue sky. A revolving scenic base, the first time such a thing had been used in the Northwest, allowed many combinations and a variety of settings. Our settings were presentational, as opposed to representational, and ideally suited to a production of this type. Scenes were changed in an average of one minute, the longest change taking only three minutes.

Owing to advance publicity, demand for reservations began to show very early. Inquiries and reservations poured in from individuals and groups up and down the coast. On February 6, 1931, the play opened. In the newspapers, it was as though a dam of newsprint had suddenly burst, gushing forth space and printers' ink. Pictures, interviews, features, rave reviews that reflected amazement at the magnitude of the undertaking—all of this gave our company an emotional lift beyond anything we could have imagined.

We added playing nights and extended the run months beyond the original dates. "Crowds Force Extension of *Peer Gynt*," ran the headlines. "*Peer Gynt* Run Record Breaker Extended Again." We were playing to standing room only, night after night, and the admission prices were $1.25 and $1.50, based on another of Burton's convictions—that people should be able to afford theatre. The production ran from February 6 to the last week in April, and we played to thirteen thousand people in our 342-seat house.

The *Christian Science Monitor*, hard-pressed to understand the unprecedented popularity of this "highbrow" play, said, "Neither the Norwegian population of Seattle nor the Grieg music could have sustained audience interest unless Ibsen had been made into a good show. This was the work of the Repertory Players . . . Not until *Peer Gynt* was it realized how great the need is in Seattle for more good spoken drama."

Audiences filling the theatre were not only from the intelligentsia or the social set. During the run of the play, a man fixing streetcar tracks in front of the theatre came to the box office for tickets. "I want my kids to see this," he explained. People in all walks of life and in all parts of the state felt the same way. Twenty years later, on the night my husband died, our daughter was being driven to the hospital in a cab. She said, "My father, Burton James, died tonight." "Burton James?" repeated the taxi driver. "I saw him in *Peer Gynt*."

The experts were loudly proclaiming that this had been the worst year in theatrical history, but for us it had been by far the best. We had increased our subscriber list to nearly three thousand and extended our season by nearly three months. In the face of the deepening Depression, the financial success of this season, which had enabled us to pay off the most pressing debts accumulated in the process of acquiring our building and installations, led us to expect future financial security—however ill-founded that expectation may have appeared in later years.

In our first season, we had an income of nearly $10,000 and a deficit of $1,358.15; in our third season, our income was over $33,000, with a deficit of $955.96. As all the money we earned went into the cost of interest on building loans and other debts, I suppose it's logical for people to wonder what the actors and producers did for money. No one was on the payroll except the stage technician, the office manager, and the janitor.

The rest of us had "day jobs" or made enough to live on as best we could.

Work in radio, which provided substantial salaries for Burton, myself, and other Playhouse people as well, tided us over the difficult months of that first year. Ultimately, we accepted austerity and tightened belts, for we enjoyed tremendous rewards. Having the opportunity to do great plays in the way we wanted to do them was compensation enough, and money never really seemed to matter too much. Our daughter once said, "You know, some of those years must have been rough, but I can't remember. We always had so much to do, and so much excitement doing it."

In the fall of 1930, my husband and I were appointed to the Drama Division of the English Department at the University of Washington. We taught two-hour laboratory courses four days a week. Mine were in actor training and Burton's in scene design and construction. We also produced all the university plays. The fact that we were working for the most part with untrained actors did not restrict us to doing plays of little importance. It was our belief that plays of merit, plays that raise important ideas, make demands on young actors that cannot be experienced in plays of no consequence.

During our time at the university, plays were produced four times a year, one in each quarter. At first, we worked in Meany Hall, cursed with a large hall with an enormous stage and awful acoustics. When the problems of trying to produce plays in such an unpromising place became too great, we rented the Playhouse to the university for a nominal sum.

In 1931, we opened our fourth season at the Playhouse. The Depression was deepening throughout the country and actors were vying with producers for places in bread lines. Actors no longer winced when telling friends, "I'm at liberty," or "I'm waiting for a part." Everybody was "waiting for a part" in some production that would bring economic life back to the nation.

It took time for us to fully realize the situation. The West Coast had not been hit as quickly as the east: the slow tremor of economic disaster had not reached Seattle in 1931–32. It was not until 1933, and the bank moratorium, that we fully understood what we were facing.

We opened our fourth season with Frederick Lonsdale's *Aren't We All?*—a charming modern comedy with taste and style. While playing *Aren't We All?*, we were in rehearsal for *Romeo and Juliet*, which we were able to produce at very little cost. We still had the sets and dress materials, wigs, tights, and shoes that had seemed fantastic extravagances when we purchased them for the second play in our first season. Now they enabled us to produce a beautiful Shakespeare, the first in our new theatre, for next to nothing.

Our next major production was Johann Wolfgang von Goethe's *Faust*, which was in rehearsal during the run of *Romeo and Juliet*. We had planned the production of

Faust as a centennial commemoration of Goethe's death and were enthusiastically supported in this by Seattle's entire German community, including the German consul, Walter Reinhardt. However, this production presented many of the same practical difficulties we had wrestled with in *Peer Gynt*. For one thing, the play was too long and had to be cut. We again had scenic backgrounds that had to be changed in the shortest time possible.

All of us delved into the historical background—the period, the author, the play itself. *Faust* has been described as a "play with a biography," meaning it had been written during the long flow of Goethe's life. Goethe, like Ibsen, was living through the social disorientation of his age, faced with the destructive reality of an industrial society. As with *Peer Gynt,* we arranged for Sunday lectures to be given by professors from the Germanic Department at the University of Washington. They dealt with *Faust* as literature and drama, as well as Goethe's philosophic approach in writing it.

We had a cast of sixty and were soon up to our necks in the extraordinary amount of work that goes into mounting a production of this kind. One Sunday morning at ten o'clock, we started arranging and lighting the sets for the eighteen scenes. At four o'clock the next morning we were still at it, when a policeman, having seen suspicious signs of activity, entered the building waving his flashlight and demanding, "All right, what goes on here?"

"We're working."

"Working? At this hour?" he responded. "My God, you've a worse job than I have." And he took himself off, shaking his head in amazement.

We opened in March to excellent reviews. On opening night, we received a cablegram of congratulation from the National Theatre in Berlin and, at a special Goethe centennial celebration held by Seattle's German community, Consul Walter Reinhardt received congratulations on the production from the Goethe-Gesellschaft and the Foreign Office in Berlin.

Faust ran from March to the middle of May. During the run, we played in Tacoma to a standing-room-only house and also in Vancouver, British Columbia. A young Seattle businessman, not a member of our board, considered *Faust* so important that he felt it should be seen in Vancouver. Touring to Tacoma, which was only thirty miles away, was quite different from transporting the entire production to Vancouver, and our budget was in no condition to permit a gamble. But the young man assured us that if we had a deficit (and we did—sixteen hundred dollars' worth), he would meet it. And he did.

Back home in Seattle, we tallied up statistics on the production. People had come from thirty towns and cities in the four western states, and young people had been brought in by bus from all around Washington. Over ten thousand people saw the twenty-five performances of the play. *Faust* did not earn the money that *Peer Gynt* did, but it garnered us a great deal of prestige. At a time when Broadway was bankrupt, *Billboard* wrote in March 1932, "The Seattle Repertory Theatre is attracting audiences from many surrounding cities in the Pacific Northwest—Oregon, California, British Columbia, and from as far away as Montana. Seattle is fortunate in having this Repertory Playhouse where this theatre finds its home."

Reviewers praised Burton as an actor and my abilities as a director. I haven't mentioned these reviews, for we were building a theatre, not ourselves. We fit only into whatever the theatre achieved. It wasn't just Burton and I who thought this way—our co-workers did as well. The success of the theatre was what counted for us. We were an oasis in a desert of cutthroat competition.

That summer we inaugurated our first summer drama festival, with a revival of *Peer Gynt, The Wild Duck,* and *A Doll's House*. During this all-Ibsen festival, we alternated performances on every day except Sundays and Mondays from June 11 through July 9. It was our first attempt at performances in repertory.

The theatre had been in existence for four years, two of them in our own building. We had survived and had paid many of the pressing debts incurred in the building process. With the productions of *Peer Gynt, Romeo and Juliet,* and *Faust,* we had achieved the shadow, if not the substance, of victory.

Talons and Clouds

The Seattle *Jewish Transcript* of October 7, 1932, predicted in its column, "The Repertory Playhouse's fifth season opening next Wednesday will draw aside curtains on the most flourishing of Repertory years." It did, but it also ushered in the shattering years of the Depression.

It had been our custom from the first years to mail season tickets to our subscribers. In 1932, the tickets were being returned with letters saying, "We can't afford season tickets this year." We began to realize the Depression was upon us, its talons sinking into our flesh.

The wounds opened and blood began to flow when we had to quitclaim our building to the owner in 1934, giving up our rights to it. At the time we were building the theatre, we had borrowed four thousand dollars from the bank, guaranteed not only by us but some members of our board. Over the years, we had managed to reduce it to fifteen hundred dollars. Then came a quarter when we could pay only the interest, then another quarter when we couldn't even meet the interest. We were threatened with the note being called.

We were out of oil and the electricity had been cut off for nonpayment of bills. We coped with the oil problem by burning odd scraps of wood in the furnace, and mollified the power company by going around to collect subrental debts that other local artists owed us for use of the theatre for concerts and recitals. We went on rehearsing, paying something here and something there. Somehow, we managed. We survived until another, more disastrous, cloud loomed.

Burton and I were employed by the Drama Department on the university campus and had been renting the Playhouse to the university for student productions. Then Glenn Hughes, head of the Drama Department, began using off-campus people for his plays, and it came to a showdown when he proposed a production of Ibsen's *Ghosts* with a retired professional actress in the leading role. We realized an Ibsen production with a nonstudent cast would be professional competition to our company and cause no end of confusion, especially in the mind of the ticket-buying public, so we refused the rental. Burton was dismissed from his university post for "noncooperation," but I stayed on. We needed the money. I continued teaching acting classes at the university and directing Associated Students of the University of Washington (ASUW) plays until 1938.

The threatening cloud of disaster began to develop shape and substance. Glenn Hughes, who was vice-president of our board of directors and thoroughly familiar with the financial crisis we faced, went to the board and said he would pay off the banknote if it would turn the theatre over to him. The board refused. Hughes then resigned, stating he disagreed with its policies.

Then it was rumoured the board of regents of the university had been approached to buy or lease our building for the Drama Department. When we heard this rumour, I went to see Dr. Leslie Ayers, dean of the law school and legal advisor to the board of regents, who was reported to be investigating the situation and the possible purchase. Dr. Ayers was a friend of ours and an interested patron of the Playhouse. He told me Hughes had informed the regents that financial difficulties would soon force us out of business and that our building would be coming up for sale. Hughes had approached the owner, who understandably would have been very willing to free himself, for hard cash, of this "specialty" building.

While I was in Dr. Ayers's office, he called a prominent member of the board of regents and said, "I have had some clarification on this business of the Playhouse and Hughes. I would advise that the board of regents not be involved." The disastrous cloud was diminished, if not dispersed, at least for the time being. This episode gave us our first indication of the lopsided competition that would develop between the state-subsidized university student theatres and the private enterprise of the Repertory Playhouse, with its adult professionals.

That fifth season we opened with Ferenc Molnár's *Liliom,* and followed it with Marianne King's *Mad, Bad and Dangerous to Know,* an original script based on the life and loves of Lord Byron. Our second Shakespeare at the Playhouse was *The Comedy of Errors,* done with the active cooperation of the high schools of Seattle. We had expanded our playing nights and were now playing Wednesday, Thursday, Friday, and Saturday, trying to perform in repertory, part of our original plan and captured in the theatre's full name.

We produced another original play that season, *Funny Man* by Al Ottenheimer. It was an amusing comedy about vaudeville and life in that kind of theatre, and the audiences enjoyed it. A local society matron played one of the leads, and it must have been with at least a touch of irony that Al noted in the log of our almost bankrupt theatre, "She comes to rehearsals in a limousine with a chauffeur who calls at the end of rehearsals for her."

In 1931, with the Depression advancing on us, we had decided to produce *Uncle Tom's Cabin.* At that time, it was considered a quaint American classic. Everybody knew of it, but few had seen it. Because eyebrows are raised today at the mention of such a "racist" play ever having been produced in our theatre, I did some research on the history of the play and the book from which it was taken. Carl Sandburg, in his biography *Abraham Lincoln: The Prairie Years*, devotes a whole chapter to *Uncle Tom's Cabin* and its author. He writes:

> As Lincoln walked the streets of Springfield and as he rode the circuit of twelve counties, living in hotels and court-houses, he met people shaken and stirred by slavery; they had read a book, the book had set their hearts on fire with hate . . . It was a hate that made them hate their own country, its laws, its flag; they believed that their own country was guilty of a crime worse than the crimes of any other country in any other time; they had read a book.*

The book was Harriet Beecher Stowe's *Uncle Tom's Cabin; or, Life among the Lowly*, published in 1852. Her book aroused anti-slavery sentiment not only in the United States but throughout the world and acted as a catalyst, unifying all the anti-slavery forces in the United States and leading to the nomination of Abraham Lincoln for president. Shortly after the novel was published, it

---

* Sandburg, Carl. *Abraham Lincoln: The Prairie Years*. Harcourt, Brace & Co., 1926.

was made into a play and played in many places for many years.

When we produced it, *Uncle Tom's Cabin*, the book that had contributed so much to the abolition of slavery, was anathema to Black Power and other forces fighting for the rights of Black people. The names Uncle Tom, Simon Legree, and Topsy are still used as stereotypes. I knew of no Black actor who had ever played the role of Uncle Tom—it was always played in blackface, and this is how Al Ottenheimer played it in our production.

We got a script of the play from Samuel French, written by G.L. Aiken. The script was a mishmash of nothing. We couldn't see how it could possibly be directed or even played. Then, one day in the midst of our dilemma, a friend called and said, "I hear you're doing *Uncle Tom's Cabin*. My mother-in-law played Topsy for twenty-six years on tour." We welcomed this miracle with open arms and rushed to see the lady. After talking to her, we understood why there was no script: the play was treated as a kind of scenario. The actors in the touring company made up lines and business to suit themselves and to fatten their parts. If it worked, and if they could get away with it, it became part of the play, but was evidently never set down in script form.

The lady we spoke with was still, at the age of seventy-six, a dynamo. She knew everyone's lines and most of the business. It was her suggestion that we have a Black male quartet to sing Little Eva into heaven, and singers and dancers for the plantation scene, which was a completely improvised musical interlude. We approached the local African Methodist Church for help and received wonderful cooperation. This was our first introduction to the Seattle Black community, and it was to lead to a long and productive friendship.

There were more than a few problems with the production, of course. One involved the scene where Eliza, with her baby in her arms, flees the "patarollers" (the dialect word for the patrols) who pursued runaway slaves, following the "drinkin' gourd" to Canada. Eliza crosses a river on the ice floes, followed by the patrols with dogs—bloodhounds.

We searched Seattle and the surrounding countryside. No bloodhounds, not even one. Though we knew that in some of the touring versions of the show spaniels, dachshunds, mongrels, and even Pekingese had been pressed into service, we wanted the scene to be exciting, not hilarious. At last, we met a man who owned a trained tracking dog, a Doberman. The owner, who was also the dog's trainer, was willing to let us have the dog for the show, under certain conditions. The dog was to come to the Playhouse in a taxi and be returned the same way.

The other stipulation was that only one person was to have anything to do with the dog. The day the owner first brought the animal to the Playhouse, he showed us why this was necessary. While the dog was lying quietly in a corner, the owner told Burton, "Grab me by my lapel." The moment Burton touched the man, the dog was up with one leap, grabbed my husband by the wrist, and held him until the owner gave him the order to release. The owner introduced the actor playing the leader of the patrol to the dog and rehearsed him in the necessary actions. He stressed that no one but this one actor was to speak to the dog or try to make friends with him. I may say that no one particularly wanted to. As an audience-pleaser, for some fond memories, and for its introduction to some fine people, *Uncle Tom's Cabin* was an important production for us.

When Paul Green's *In Abraham's Bosom* won the Pulitzer Prize for its New York production in 1932, we asked for and received permission to produce it at the Playhouse. The play's story is laid in the turpentine camps of North Carolina in 1885. Though the Emancipation Proclamation had freed the slaves two decades earlier, peonage still existed. Abraham is the illegitimate son of the white landowner and half-brother to his father's white son. An altercation arises between the boys, and the father whips his Black son to show him his place and to teach him that he can't "get uppity" with a white man. "You've got to know your place, Abe, and I've got to teach you." But Abe never accepts this. He hopes for something better than being a turpentine hand in peonage and longs for an education that could lift him out of the hopelessness of his life. His struggle goes on until he is lynched.

The play needed a Black cast with only two white actors. In order to cast it, we went back to the African Methodist Church. We got not only a cast but a choir and started rehearsal early in October. All the cast, with the exception of Joseph S. Jackson, who played Abraham, and Sara Oliver, who played his mother, were from the North, and some had been born in Seattle. The area and situations of the play were almost totally foreign to them. Mr. Jackson, however, came from within a few miles of the play's location, and Mrs. Oliver had lived in that area. Although Mr. Jackson had been in the North for years, he had not forgotten his early roots. And Mrs. Oliver still spoke as the people in the play spoke, and she knew the customs and behaviour patterns of the people in the area where she was born and raised. Her business with the snuff stick, her prayers, her dancing in moments of joy gave a lively authenticity to the scenes she was in and seemed to communicate itself to the other members of the cast.

The play opened January 11, 1933. Reviewers, excited by the performance given by these Black amateurs, called it "the greatest triumph of The Playhouse." Audiences came from up and down the coast to see it, many asking where the actors had come from, although most of them had lived in Seattle all their lives. Suddenly, the papers, which at that time would not print photographs of Black people but only line drawings, were calling the actors "Seattle artists." Audiences gave them standing ovations and shouted "Bravo!" (rare experiences for Seattle) and left the Playhouse as though it were a church.

In the spring of 1933, remembering our financial successes with *Peer Gynt* and *Faust,* we decided to produce Gerhart Hauptmann's *The Sunken Bell,* orchestra and all. But all the support from the German community seemed to have disappeared. A strange new wind was blowing in the world: Hitler had come to power. The production was incredibly beautiful to look at but a crashing bore. We didn't realize it at the time, but with the changing world situation, as well as our straitened financial circumstances, we were moving into the period of the realistic play.

We were able to start rehearsals on our fall production without quite as many austerities as the year before, although we still owed money to the oil and electricity people and wouldn't have heat or light until we settled the accounts.

In our fifth season, we had acquired a small building directly adjacent to the Playhouse for our apprentice classes and extra rehearsal space. We were particularly glad to have the apprenticeship building at this point, because it was hooked up to another electric light company, one to which we were not indebted. We strung a cable over to the theatre and jerry-rigged one light on the stage and one in the workshop. That was the situation in September of 1933.

We opened our sixth season with Björnstjerne Björnson's *Love and Geography,* a charming Norwegian comedy. We followed this with *Richard III*, our third Shakespeare. There was growing interest in these Shakespearean performances in the city's high schools. More high schools sent larger numbers of students, and these performances increased our receipts at the box office, which for us was an important consideration.

We went on producing plays and attending meetings and overcoming crises, one after another. By May of 1934, we had been unable to raise the money to meet two payments on the banknote and the royalty for our current play was in arrears. The licence inspector was protesting because we hadn't paid the city theatrical licence, due the previous November. There was also a suit instituted by the National Discount Corporation against Sam Fitz (our landlord), his deceased wife's estate, and the Playhouse, for our neon signs, of which there were two. On top of that, we had two other suits threatened. We sent our irate creditors ten dollars apiece and crossed our fingers for luck.

Other forces, nationwide in scope, were at work shaping the course that our group was to take. We received a letter from the State Transient Service, which argued the case of the recreational needs of the homeless and dispossessed of the area. Most of the transients who were wandering the nation in search of jobs and security were under twenty-five, in and out of jail, following the seasonal harvest work when there was any to be had. At that time, they had no organization interested in their daily problems or able to give them the "respectable" poverty represented by organized charity.

The State Transient Service director's letter sketched some of the most pertinent facts:

> Due to the pressure of many perplexing problems that confound us in relief administration from week to week, we have found it difficult to make adequate recreational provision for these people as a group and hence this letter to you. I would ask whether you and your associates would be willing, within the coming months of September and October, to arrange for a definite evening's entertainment for the benefit of these people . . . The drab and colorless life led by these people tends to provoke irrationalism and I am of the opinion that if your organization could co-operate with us, as suggested above, that your organization would be making a fine contribution to public service. We are confronted with a rather serious situation in dealing with this group of people who are anxious to return to work and still are denied such an opportunity. It is pertinent, therefore, to endeavor to give them, within the limitations of reason, some of the things the average person has come to regard over a period of years as a standard of human recreation and daily life.

We had no time to arrange special programs, but we could make seats available in the theatre and we did. The street railway was willing to honour transfers for return fares, so all the transients had to pay was the tax on admission.

We finished the season with *Volpone*, adapted by Stefan Zweig from Ben Jonson's script, and we had some censorship problems. There is a scene in the play where Volpone attempts to rape Columba and there is a scream from her window, "Rape! Rape!" We left it in. The Pasadena Community Theatre had changed the line to "Skulduggery! Skulduggery!" but we felt this was terribly hard to scream and somewhat lacking in accuracy.

In 1933, the country was moving into the darkest depth of the Depression. The ceremonies for Franklin Delano Roosevelt's inauguration in 1933 had hardly been concluded when a run started on the banks back east and travelled with electrifying speed across the country. President Roosevelt declared a bank moratorium from March 3 to 14 and all banks closed. We had been playing *In Abraham's Bosom* to standing-room-only houses since January, the best sales we had had in a long time. The day of the moratorium, as fast as the office staff could lift the telephone, they received cancellations. The only money people had was in their wallets, and no one knew when "normalcy" would be restored. It broke the back of our successful run, but as the Irish say, "When God closes one door, He opens another." The door that opened for us then was the Negro Repertory under the WPA—the Works Progress Administration.

President Roosevelt set up agencies in government to try to stem the tide of despair and depression that was dragging the country under. One of these agencies was the Works Progress Administration, directed by Harry Hopkins. The WPA included a section known as the Federal Arts Project that was to deal with all the arts as artists in every category were out of work. Hallie Flanagan of the Vassar College Drama Department was in charge of theatre. When we discovered this was not to be a "pork barrel" for Broadway and Hollywood, we prepared a brief for what we decided to call a Negro Repertory Company. In order to participate in the Arts Project, our theatre had to provide rehearsal space and theatre space for playing dates and all the physical equipment for production, staging, costumes, and scenery. In the beginning, the government paid salaries only to those on relief, enabling them to earn money with their skills instead of receiving a dole for doing nothing. Money earned by productions would go into a cashier's fund and could be used for royalties, rents, and equipment.

When the Arts Project was set up, our proposal was accepted. There was a considerable delay in getting started, hindered by the red tape that governments wind around such endeavours, but we were finally given the go-ahead signal. There were supervisors and managers but no people—as yet.

One day, the state supervisor of the project called my husband. "Burton, don't you need the money? Get on the project. Come down and sign the payroll."

"I will when you send us the people. Where are they? I work for my money."

We had applied in April 1935, but it was not until September that we began work on André Obey's *Noah,* a story of Noah and his animals and the Flood. We used Black music and introduced Black dancing to express the jubilation of Noah and his family when the Flood recedes. The cast and chorus gave a very good show. Reviewers expressed amazement at the talent displayed by people "taken from the scrap-heap of unemployment." The reviewer in the *Seattle Star* commented, "This all-Negro cast put on a performance so rich, so full of promise, it was tragic in its implications. Tragic because these people who have so much to contribute have so long been wasted."

Our next play, *Stevedore,* by Paul Peters and George Sklar, was in rehearsal while *Noah* was playing. It was a controversial play about a strike on the New Orleans waterfront and one of our board members resigned over it, saying he thought the production was very good but it gave people ideas—ideas he could not accept. The ideas he found so onerous were those evoked by the bitter struggle sometimes necessary to build a union, a situation not unknown in Seattle and San Francisco, as well as New Orleans.

Very early in this project, we recognized the dearth of good plays for Black casts, so we began writing our own. After *Stevedore*, we created a musical revue called *Swing, Gates, Swing*, and Theodore Browne, an excellent actor, began writing a play about John Henry, a Black railroad worker who lost his life trying to compete with a steel drill. He called the play *Natural Man*.

We began to arrange Aristophanes's *Lysistrata* for production. We placed it in Ethiopia, as Mussolini was developing his war techniques there for later use in Spain, so the country was somewhat familiar to our audiences. We were in dress rehearsal and just about to open when a major from San Francisco expressed horror to the state supervisor and state director of our project that the WPA would permit production of such a bawdy play. This project always seemed to be involved with military men in one capacity or another. I sometimes wished that somebody would put me in charge of some military operation—I figured I knew just as much about the military as these military men did about the theatre.

A meeting was called. We asked how they could know what they were censoring if they hadn't seen it. Don Abel, state supervisor of the WPA, sent his wife and his secretary to the opening. Another meeting was called the next day. Mr. Abel reported that his wife and secretary said the play was "indecent and bawdy." My husband retorted, "My wife directed that play. Does that mean that my wife's tastes are 'indecent and bawdy,' or that your wife doesn't know anything about theatre and in any event shouldn't be permitted to censor productions?" Aristophanes's two-thousand-year-old comedy, which had opened at the Moore Theatre to capacity audiences, was summarily closed in the best interest of the Federal Theatre Project.

Our cast and chorus were all Black, but there had been some white people on the project: our stage technician, electrician, and the costume and scene designers. Burton had to explain to the supervisor when we started that these were trained theatre people and essential to the project, even if they were white. When we needed white actors in the cast, we got them from the white theatre project or used actors from our theatre. We had to get them accepted by the supervisors, although white actors also needed relief.

The people involved in the white project of the WPA were largely from vaudeville. One of them was Toby Leitch, an elderly man who had been in every kind of theatre known—tent shows, carnivals, medicine shows, circuses, and Toby Shows, which is where he got his name. I first directed him when he played the white boss in *Stevedore*. During the early rehearsals, he seemed to be paying very little attention to the script.

When I reminded him that his lines had to be learned by a certain date, he said, aghast, "You mean I have to memorize all those lines? Don't think I can. Never memorized a line in my life." Amazed, I asked, "But what did you and the other actors in your shows do?" He said, "Just made 'em up. Depended on the audience. If they wanted comic, they got comic. If they wanted serious, we gave 'em serious."

The language in *Stevedore* was a little rough in spots. One of the women in the cast had to say, "I got the red-headed son-of-a-bitch!" She did not think she ought to say the line and consulted her pastor. He told her it was all right—she was not saying it, the character in the play was. Toby was shocked too. He said, "We could never get away with any language like that in our shows, but then this is an Art Theatre."

The success of the Black group was creating friction with the white group, which was doing vaudeville turns in the parks. Annoyed by the publicity the Black group was getting, it began complaining to Washington that white professionals, some of whom were members of the Actor's Equity Association, were being denied opportunities that Black amateurs were getting. So I was asked to take over the white group as well and produce the Living Newspaper, *Power*.

The Living Newspaper was a type of play in documentary form developed under the WPA. The first production was called *The Plow That Broke the Plains*, a film by Pare

Lorentz, with music by Virgil Thomson. It was a story of pioneering the Midwest and the breaking up of the grasslands that resulted in the dust bowls. *Power* had to do with the growing interest in the government's development of electric power through the Tennessee Valley Authority and the Boulder Dam, and it was a natural for our area in Washington, which was very power conscious and in the process of building the Ross Dam. I left the Black project for the time being and tackled *Power*. I was staggered when I saw the script. There was everything in it—actors playing scenes, film, slides, a chorus, and an orchestra to play Lee Wainer's music.

We got the rehearsals going. If I had had problems with untrained Black amateurs, I had even more problems with white professionals. One man came up to me and asked what mugs I wanted him to use. I didn't know what he was talking about. He explained patiently that he had forty-six mugs and wanted me to see them so I could tell him which ones to use. It turned out he was referring to the roster of facial expressions that had been his stock-in-trade as a performer. I told him he should memorize his lines and say them, and the mug he wore every day would be just fine.

When we were in dress rehearsal, the slides that had been sent to us cracked, one after another. The operator told me they were for older projection machines and the present lamps were too hot for them. A man who happened to be working at some odd job backstage said to me, "I can make you some slides that won't crack in that machine. I used to do the slides for the songs they sang in the old motion picture houses on skid road." So I gave him a copy of the script, indicated what slides were needed, and he took off. A day or two later, he came back with beautiful slides, some of them coloured, which did not crack and were far better than the ones that had been sent to us. He also became our photographer and got remarkable pictures working with an old-fashioned camera and flashlight arrangement, retouching the negatives. One day, I got a call from the state director, who was trying to find out if we had been splurging on new photographic equipment. He'd had a complaint from Washington, DC, about our pictures, "because they're too good!"

Another positive development that grew out of this chaos was the contribution made by the Black group to the white production. We needed a chorus, prop people, and trained stage managers. By now, some members of the Black group were pretty good technicians, as well as fine actors, and I got permission from the directors of the project to put the Black group on this production. They came over willingly, joyfully, and everybody worked together, whites taking orders from Black stage managers and technicians, Blacks working amicably with whites—no Black Power, no white power, no tensions, no frictions anywhere, just people joined in the effort of doing a job and doing it well.

The experience of discovering talents among people who had been doing dull, mundane jobs was a constant source of joy to us. To see the colossal waste of such human resources, the most valuable assets to any country, and to realize what could have been accomplished and what this accomplishment could have meant was staggering. In 1969, burned-out cities were being rebuilt all over the country—even in Washington, DC—at a tremendous cost to the taxpayer. Contrast this outlay with the few million dollars originally given to the federal arts programs. It seems that we can find money for just about anything and everything but people.

We all dreamed of a permanent Federal Arts Project, with a Cabinet minister representing all the arts. In the WPA, set up for relief in a stressful time, there were dancers, painters, architects, writers, playwrights, directors, and actors. Orson Welles's Mercury Theatre was one of the projects. It was said that 85 percent of the paintings on display at the New York World's Fair had been done on WPA. When, later, some of these paintings were to be sent abroad, Congress objected—they had been done on WPA, so of course they were "Communistic."

How did the newspapers view all this activity in the theatre? With a jaundiced eye! The *Seattle Post-Intelligencer* and the *Seattle Times* opposed President Roosevelt and his policies and the theatre presented a ready target. This was apparently true for newspapers throughout the country. When we presented Sinclair

Lewis's play, *It Can't Happen Here,* with the Black group, it drew a blast from the local papers and others, east to west. What seemed to be controversial was the theme of the play; that fascism can happen here. All through the rehearsals, we were getting word from Washington: "Cut this speech." "Add this." "Take out that." We finally had to throw caution to the winds and do the play as Lewis wrote it. The play, part of the Federal Theatre Project, opened in eighteen cities on the same evening—the first and only time in theatre history this had happened.

We seemed to be constantly involved in one problem or another on this project, as the red tape wound tighter and politicians got into the act. At the start, we had one timekeeper, a young Black woman who was a University of Washington graduate. Every two weeks, I signed her time sheet and submitted it. By the end of the project, we had three timekeepers, political appointees. Essential people had been dropped from the project to make room for them.

The people on the project were to start work at 10:00 a.m. and stop at 4:00 p.m. I learned about inflexible bureaucracy the hard way when a supervisor came by and found the group in rehearsal on a difficult bit of business after 4:00 p.m. Against the protests of cast and chorus, I had to dismiss them summarily. At the beginning of the project, the organizers graded people as skilled or unskilled and paid them accordingly. In view of the fact they were all unskilled, such a situation would have created no end of dissension, so my husband had to straighten it out. They were paid sixty-six dollars a month, later raised to seventy-two. Directors and technicians were first paid seventy-two dollars and later ninety-six dollars a month.

We all learned a great deal. I had never known, before I worked on the project, how easy it was for Black people to become involved with the police. Although we never had any really serious problems, it seemed that practically every day someone was missing from the cast or crew, picked up by a police dragnet. I never met so many plainclothesmen in my life, and I got to know some quite well. The police could hold Black suspects for twenty-four hours and then had to charge them or let them go, which meant they would lose a day's pay. I remember with gratitude one policeman who would call and tell me he had brought in so-and-so but would see if he could get him released so he would only lose half a day's pay. In that day, Black people had to take it in their stride—not today, not anymore. I remember one of the fellows on the project who simply shrugged and said, "Oh, they pick me up whether I'm wearing dungarees or my ice cream pants."

My connection with the WPA came to an end when I became so tied up in red tape devised by the administration that I was spending most of my time and energy in controversy over this and that rather than producing plays. I resigned. In 1936, the United States was pulling out of the Depression. The Second World War looked imminent, and people were beginning to get jobs creating "the tools to finish the job," as Winston Churchill said in one of his speeches.* The WPA was getting the axe, and the first project to be hit in the pocket was the theatre. Anything and everything connected with it seemed to be controversial, and Congress had yowled loud and long about wasting taxpayers' money on the arts.

We met the crises of the distressful years of the Depression and enjoyed the excitement of the excellent work done by the Black people on the project. We maintained our concern for the development of programs for our young audiences. We re-evaluated our approach to the theatre, economically, philosophically, and artistically. Along with the intensive activity and pressures of work in the theatre, we became concerned with the lengthening shadows of war moving across the face of the world, with Mussolini's aggression in Ethiopia, Hitler and Mussolini in Spain, and the Japanese invasion of Manchuria.

As Hitler, that "madman with a mission," moved from the Anschluss in Austria to the takeover in Czechoslovakia and threats to Poland, our apprehension increased. But we were totally involved in Spain. We participated in programs to raise money for ambulances, medical

* From Winston Churchill's London broadcast from February 9, 1941: "Give us the tools, and we will finish the job."

supplies, everything, for the money of Republican Spain was frozen in the United States. The American government was following the British and French policy of nonintervention. A group called America First, organized by Charles Lindbergh and Senator Burton K. Wheeler, actively opposed any involvement in the Spanish Civil War, but the American people were generally critical of this policy and young people were intensely concerned.

One day, one of my students came to the Playhouse and asked to see me. He explained, "I have to talk to somebody. I won't be in class tomorrow, because I'm leaving tonight for Paris. I'm joining the Abraham Lincoln Brigade to fight in Spain. My parents would never understand." And they didn't. When his father found out, he commented bitterly, "And that's the guy who objected to being in ROTC on campus because he hates uniforms and the military. And now he's off to fight in another man's war three thousand miles away!"

Two of my students and a friend left for Spain, and one was killed at Teruel. The Madrileños, when they saw the ranks of young men marching through the streets of bombed Madrid, cheered wildly, crying, "We are not alone!" Years later, when the Second World War had erupted and the United States was involved, President Roosevelt admitted his policy on Spain had been a mistake.

Remembering those days, and the Federal Theatre Project, years, miles, and a new country later, I am filled again with dismay at the stupidity of people who can get themselves elected to positions of power that enable them to arbitrate the destinies of others, often without thought or consideration. Hallie Flanagan told the story of a congressman who called her the day after the vote in Congress that killed the Federal Theatre Project. He wanted to get his niece on the project. Miss Flanagan told him there was no longer any Ferderal Theatre Project, that Congress had just killed it. The congressman said, "Oh. Was that what we voted down yesterday?"

The dreams we had had of a permanent Federal Arts Project vanished for good in the "mushroom cloud" of the Second World War. It was spreading fast along the horizon.

Off to the USSR

To go back a bit, early in the spring of 1934, we had been amazed to receive an announcement of theatre festivals to be held at Malvern and Stratford in England and in Moscow during the first ten days in September. When in our lives had a government anywhere thought it important to present a festival in theatre? And what kind of a festival could the USSR present? Had we not read in the newspapers that art, as well as artists, had been liquidated by the Workers' Republic as something too contemptibly bourgeois for the high ideals and development of a Communist state?

We had long recognized the advantages of being able to do freely what we wanted to do in the theatre in this faraway corner of the country, but we also recognized the disadvantages of being so far removed from opportunities of seeing what other theatres were doing. I had often looked at some play I had directed and thought it good, but I longed for some more objective comparison and criticism. So, with the announcements of the Malvern Festival, the Shakespearean Festival in Stratford, England, and, most exciting of all, this festival in Moscow, marvellous opportunities were being offered for a very rich theatre experience—if only one could go. But we were deep in the Depression in 1934, and such expenditure didn't seem possible. Just about this time, I received word that my father's estate—he had died in the fall of 1933—was to be settled. There was very little in the estate, as he had lost everything in the Depression. But Burton said to me, "When you get that money, take it and go to England and Russia to see those festivals. There isn't enough for both of us to go, but you go. It will do us all good."

Marianne King, who had written two plays for us, decided she would like to accompany me. Many of our friends thought we were insane to think of taking a trip to the Soviet Union. I received my twelve hundred dollars from Father's estate and Marianne and I set out. When we got to Chicago, the city was in an uproar. We had arrived on the day the gangster John Dillinger was shot.

When we were preparing for our trip, the agent at American Express urged us to take the German ship *Bremen,* on which we could travel first class for what it would cost us for second class on the Cunard line. We said no. Mussolini had been at work in Ethiopia and we suspected Hitler's intentions, though he hadn't yet revealed them in Spain. While we weren't too well informed about what was going on, we didn't like what we did know, and we certainly didn't want to travel on a German ship. We were what was later called "prematurely anti-fascist."

We spent a lovely two weeks in England, seeing the festivals at Malvern and in the beautiful new theatre at Stratford, as well as plays in London. Early one morning, we boarded the *Siber*, a Russian ship bound for Leningrad and Moscow. We sailed down the Thames, out through the North Sea, and passed through the Kiel Canal by moonlight. Not many people were travelling to the Soviet Union then. President Roosevelt had just extended recognition to this socialist government, having waited about the same length of time it had taken Catherine II of Russia to recognize the United States after the American Revolution. The American Revolution shook every throne in Europe; the Russian Revolution shook the world.

The trip had been paid for in advance and arranged by Intourist—hotel rooms, sightseeing tours, theatre tickets, and a Russian guide who spoke English with an American accent and used American slang. When I asked where she had learned it, she said, "I work for an American road-building firm, and this is my vacation." Things had to be arranged this way, of course, since we couldn't spend any foreign currency in the country and weren't allowed to buy Russian money.

Before we landed at Leningrad, someone said, "Watch your belongings. They'll steal you blind." We made a mental note. I decided when we docked that Leningrad had the smell of Seattle—lumber and the sea. We were taken to the Hotel Europa and given, much to our amazement, fabulous accommodations. It began to look as if things might turn out all right after all. Later that night I discovered that, in the excitement of arrival and customs, I had left my coat in the Immigration Pavilion. The next morning, I spoke to our guide about it. She dismissed my concern with a casual, "It will be at the hotel when we return from the sightseeing tour." And it was. I erased my mental note about people stealing me blind.

In Leningrad we visited the Winter Palace and the Hermitage Museum with its fabulous collection of paintings and art objects, St. Isaac's Cathedral with its great malachite pillars, and then an anti-religious museum. It wasn't really so much anti-religious as it was anti-superstition, an attempt to eradicate by education the reverence for the most revolting objects that had held the uneducated people of this big country in thrall for centuries. It was at this museum that we saw women soldiers on guard for the first time.

The material things we saw didn't interest us as much as the people we met and talked to, the history, the impressive beauty of the old and the driving energy of the new. Moscow was being built and rebuilt, the subway was under construction, streets were being widened.

Everything seemed to be moving at an accelerated pace, and everywhere was the slogan for "Work and Defense."

We arrived in Moscow on September 1, a holiday similar to our Labour Day, but this holiday was for youth. Returning from a sightseeing tour, we passed streets where marchers stood preparing for a parade to be held in the evening when work was over. On one street, we saw masses of men and women in work clothes, large boutonnieres of red flowers in their coat lapels, the men carrying guns. "Who are they?" we wanted to know. "Just militia men," the guide replied.

Some years after my trip, my husband and I were teaching at the University of British Columbia summer school. Hitler had just invaded the Soviet Union. At dinner one evening, another American teaching with us said, "Well, this is the end of the Soviet Union. Hitler will be in Moscow in six weeks." I startled the table by announcing, with conviction, "Hitler will never get to Moscow. Every man, woman, and child will rise up against him. He's making the same mistake Napoleon made. It's the end of Hitler, not the end of the Soviet Union." Our co-worker laughed. "I was at a dinner party before I left Washington. I was the only one in civvies. Those military men said, 'Hitler will go through Russia like a hot knife through butter.' They should know!"

I don't know what the American military were seeing in 1934, or what anyone else saw, but I based my opinions on what I had seen for myself.

One of our most interesting experiences was when we were taken, as part of a large group of festival participants, to meet a Mr. Vontsky, assistant commissar of the theatre. Theatres were under the Commissariat of Education. When asked if the Russian theatres were censored, he said, "Assuredly. We censor immorality, religion, counter-revolution, and mysticism. No classic is censored, and any play that seems to have merit is first produced before a decision to censor is made. Even though it may contain one or all of the censorable elements, it may have other values which offset the censorable defects."

Throughout the festival, we had been very interested in the audiences that thronged the theatres we attended, obviously working men and women, people who in the old regime could not walk the streets in the areas where the theatres were located, much less enter one of them. Some of the skeptics in our group scoffed at the crowded houses. "Naturally, the Soviet government wouldn't have festival guests attending a theatre with a half-empty house." The inference was that these audiences had been rounded up and sent to the theatre at bayonet-point, or with some other dire threat, to create a good impression on foreign theatregoers. However, when I made a last-minute switch in plans, I found that that theatre was crowded too. If I had believed it was for my personal benefit, I would have been awestruck at the efficiency that could fill a theatre on a few hours' notice, and flattered that they had considered me of sufficient importance to go to such lengths to impress me.

About 50 percent of the plays we saw might have been classed as propaganda, but even they had so much that was excellent theatre, were so beautifully acted, and achieved such distinction in production that we, who had too little background to be moved by the propaganda, sat enthralled. We had long believed that theatre had a contribution to make in helping to make education exciting and could provide emotional content that would interest and excite the viewer, leaving indelible impressions. Theatres were being built in the Soviet Union not only to fill needs but to create them.

While producing contemporary plays, the Russian theatre we saw did not neglect the classics, either its own or those of other countries. One of our most delightful evenings was spent at the Second Moscow Art, watching a performance of Shakespeare's *Twelfth Night*. In an address of welcome, one of the directors of the theatre said, "We have a feeling of healthy confidence which goes well with the life and colour of Shakespeare and the vigour of his sonorous voice." At some point during the production, a young Englishman in our group turned to me and whispered, "I think nobody but the English should produce Shakespeare." I replied, "After seeing the productions at Stratford, I think anybody *but* the English should produce Shakespeare!"

Probably the most interesting experience we had in theatre while in Moscow was our visit to a production of the Moscow Theatre for Children. What interested us most was the company's understanding of the child's psychological need to participate in the experience of theatre. During intermissions, the young audience, under supervision, danced, sang, and drew pictures. Every child is stimulated by the theatre to do something on his or her own and wants to actively create.

Our curiosity was insatiable. At the Kremlin Museum we saw the antiquities of the old regime, jewelled harnesses and weapons, solid gold stirrups and gem-trimmed saddles, clothing embroidered in gold and silver thread, encrusted with pearls and other precious stones. We saw Lenin in his glass coffin, and I noted that he was a rather short man, dressed in a simple soldier's uniform, with small, delicate hands.

One day, a Scots doctor in our party asked, "Would you ladies care to see a propholactoria for prostitutes?" We figured we were on the tour to be educated, so we answered, "Yes. What is it?" The propholactoria turned out to be a rehabilitation centre that provided hospital services and education: training in all kinds of skills for factory work, even instruction in driving tractors. The administrator of the institution told us there were over thirty thousand women engaged in prostitution in the city of Moscow. They knew the exact number because the women had to be registered with the police and carry permits. Women came to the institution voluntarily and could leave at will. Prostitution was not a crime, but anyone profiting from these women was considered a criminal. Few women who entered the institution left before they had been trained for other jobs.

I must stress that our visit to Russia was in 1934. The Russians felt their revolution had survived the Allied intervention that followed and was now consolidated. My friend Marianne and her sister returned to Russia again in 1936 and told me later that everything had changed. Sergei Kirov had been assassinated late in 1934, and the Moscow Trials were beginning. In 1936, Marianne said, they received courteous but perfunctory attention. No one was making friends with foreigners.

We left the Soviet Union after our ten-day visit exhilarated and exhausted because we had seen and done so much but also depressed by the future we could see looming, given the gathering clouds of the Second World War. Emperor Haile Selassie had pleaded his cause fruitlessly to the League of Nations. The world seemed to be in the grip of those who based their actions not on realities but on their hopes, which were fantasies. They were blind to reality: everyone who had anything but butterflies in the head could not fail to see the outcome of such a confrontation, not only for those immediately involved but for the entire world.

After I had recovered from the exhaustion and excitement of the trip, I began to sort out my impressions. In

England, it seemed to me the theatres were dull, doing plays that said "nothing to nobody," and which, because of their content, were given dull, unexciting productions. Even at Stratford, Shakespearean performances were pedestrian and conventional. In the Soviet Union, on the other hand, many of the plans we had for our own theatre seemed to be in the process of realization. The recognition that theatre was an essential need for the many, not a frill for the few, and the efforts to extend it to remote areas, the work being done for the children, and the efforts being made to involve this young audience in the creative process all impressed and informed me. I thought of something Lincoln Steffens once said when he returned from the Soviet Union shortly after the revolution: "I have seen the future, and it works." Then as now, it is not, of course, given to any of us to foretell how far any given future will extend, nor how long its exciting promises will last. My glimpse into a possible future took place in 1934. The future of that day now lies far in the past, and I am sad to say that many of mankind's hopes lie with it.

The Rise and Fall of the Washington State Theatre

At the inception of the Repertory Playhouse, we decided that, as a community theatre, we had a responsibility to the young people of the city. We realized that with nothing but movies to watch (the "talkies" were coming on strong), a whole generation could have no experience of the live actor and the living theatre.

When we built our own theatre, one of the factors that inclined us toward building in the university district, one block from the university campus, was the expectation that the University of Washington, with its more than eight thousand students at that time, would provide a potential audience. But that didn't happen, even though the *University of Washington Daily*, the campus newspaper, reviewed the plays favourably and sometimes with considerable enthusiasm.

We concluded that students, not having had any experience of live theatre, had very little interest in it. If we wanted to correct this attitude, where would we start?

We decided to go to the high schools. We thought if we could introduce the state's high school students, at that time some ninety-five thousand individuals, to theatre, and keep at it for a reasonable length of time, a positive attitude toward theatre could be developed. When we produced *Romeo and Juliet*, we approached the school authorities, as Shakespeare was in the high school curriculum. These authorities were naturally hesitant about taking such a precedent-setting step, but they did agree to a limited experiment—a special weekday matinee for high school students, played during school time. The results of the experiment were a revelation in the eagerness of the students who thronged to the performances and their response in the theatre and in the classroom.

By 1935–36, these performances had grown to include every high school and junior high school in Seattle, as well as many separate and private schools; 10,673 students attended the thirty school matinees that season. Then students started coming in from outlying towns. Sometimes a hundred would come a distance of a hundred miles or so in chartered buses, and it seemed that many more would come if they could afford it.

Early in 1935, a couple of out-of-town tours were proposed as an experiment. As finances were extremely limited (thanks to the Depression), the Playhouse undertook this touring at its own risk. We played Shakespeare's *A Midsummer Night's Dream* with a cast of fifty, including a ballet corps of twelve and a ten-piece orchestra of first-chair members of the Seattle Symphony performing Mendelssohn's incidental music. We played three matinees in Tacoma and two in Everett to capacity audiences.

The enthusiasm of the student audiences for *A Midsummer Night's Dream* indicated to the committee that the time seemed ripe to extend this theatre-going experience to other high schools in the state. When a pledge of the State Board's interest and assistance had been obtained, the Playhouse presented a brief and a budget to the Rockefeller Foundation for a grant of $35,000 to initiate the project as a three-year experiment. The foundation had to be assured of two things: the continued interest of the State Board and the standard of our productions.

On April 15, 1936, the Rockefeller Foundation gave us a grant of $35,000 to establish a theatre for the high schools of the state, to be called the Washington State Theatre. We received $20,000 of the grant in 1936 to finance office space and meet other expenses involved in setting up the project, in 1937–38, we received $10,000, and in 1939–40, the final $5,000.

We decided to open the tour with Shakespeare's *The Comedy of Errors*, a riotous farce that could appeal to the most unsophisticated members of the audience. Some of those from the schools on the committee thought

Shakespeare would not interest the students. One man said, "Students are bored with Shakespeare. We are trying to take it out of the curriculum as soon as possible." His opinion notwithstanding, we stuck with Shakespeare. This was to be a theatre for education.

We felt that Shakespeare could be more satisfactorily introduced in the schools before our production with the use of lesson plans that gave the students information about the cast of characters, their relationships, and so on. In every instance where they were used we had a more responsive audience.

A staggering amount had to be accomplished before the opening tour. Promotional and publicity material was designed to appeal to a wide range in the potential audiences. Press and radio releases were prepared for the newspapers and radio stations near the playing centres. People who had worked with us for a number of years provided the staff and personnel for this new venture.

All members of the group performed in more than one capacity: the two advance men who arranged the tours also acted in the company for which they had prepared the way. Another kept a critical eye on the performances and his reports resulted in some distinct changes in our approaches to acting and directing.

We realized that actors might still be regarded in some areas as "mountebanks and scalawags," so rules of conduct were agreed upon. No smoking was permitted in or around school buildings and, of course, no liquor was allowed at any time. It is interesting to note that these rules were strictly observed by everybody from truck drivers to cast and crew. Later, letters from school people and hotelkeepers testified to the validity of our approach.

Another step in preparing for this and subsequent tours was a trip by Al Ottenheimer to high schools in the state in advance of the playing dates, speaking to school assemblies. Al's talks provided an exciting introduction to theatre for a new, inexperienced audience, and his engaging manner of presentation appealed to the young people, for it was humorous, informal, and unpretentious.

While all this preparation was going on, rehearsals were in progress for *The Comedy of Errors*. The Washington State Theatre opened its first tour in Aberdeen, Washington, on November 2, 1936, with a matinee for students and an evening performance for adults. That first tour, we performed in nineteen playing centres, drawing from 143 outlying communities, and about thirty-five thousand students and adults saw the play. Student prices were twenty-five cents, adults fifty and seventy-five cents. Student tickets were sold in the schools, while adult performances were sponsored, and the PTA and other service groups handled ticket sales.

We received support and encouragement from a wonderful variety of sources. Without exception, unions everywhere supported us in generous measure, largely unprompted, and gave us special consideration in the matters of wage scales, hours, conditions of work, and general helpfulness. Their support and encouragement were greatly appreciated during the Washington State Theatre tours.

At the conclusion of the first tour, the play choice committee decided that the second tour should be a modern play, *No More Frontier*, the story of the pioneering of Idaho. The play seemed a natural for young audiences, with cattle rustlers, cowboys, and Indians, but we found that much of the play's tragic element was beyond the experience of the youngsters. The adult audiences, on the other hand, appreciated *No More Frontier* more than they did *The Comedy of Errors*. We frequently heard people in the audience sobbing aloud, as they remembered their bitter experiences as pioneers.

To ease the wait between acts, we engaged a musical director who travelled with the company and conducted student players, using a musical score that had been sent to any school with an orchestra two weeks before the playing date. School orchestras entered into the experience enthusiastically, for they became part of the performance. This was our first attempt to involve the theatre with other arts that already existed in the school.

In our efforts to find plays that met the interests and needs of this young audience, the play choice committee circulated forty-five contemporary scripts to students, teachers, and school superintendents. We were unable to find anything they didn't class as either silly or cheap. My husband decided plays that were contemporaneously valid and suitable would have to be specially written. But then he came up with another, better, idea: to create a situation that would permit the students to write their own plays. With this in mind, he approached West Seattle High School to put a class in playwriting into its curriculum, to be conducted during school time. A class in creative writing became a reality in a Seattle high school.

One of the students kept a verbatim record of the discussions Burton held with the class to determine the interests of the young people before they put pen to paper. They thought at first that fascism might be a subject, but then they decided that democracy would be a better subject, as they were more familiar with that. They decided to call the play *Search* and to create it in the form of the Living Newspaper.

Before the play was completed, the term was over. During summer vacation, the students came to the Playhouse and finished their play. It was produced, along with other one-acts, in the fall tour of the Washington State Theatre. The audiences, though unfamiliar with the form, were enthusiastic about the content. *Search* released a previously scarcely tapped stream of creative energy and ability and in the process made a significant legacy to teaching techniques.

While we broke even financially at the end of our first year of operation, definite deficiencies in budget planning began to emerge. Even the twenty-five-cent admission was too much for many students. In this day of "student affluence," it's hard to believe that many students then did not have a twenty-five-cent piece.*

But that was the situation, caused by the effects of the countrywide recession on the state of Washington. The Sino-Japanese War had curtailed and almost wiped out the chief market for the state's lumbering, Asia. First pulp and saw mills, then logging camps shut down, and the maritime trades, shipping and longshoring, were keenly affected. In the great apple orchards in eastern Washington, there was a plethora of fruit. Some farmers had thousands of dollars' worth of unsalable fruit in warehouses or rotting on the ground yet did not have enough money to buy groceries for their families.

For the first production of the Washington State Theatre's second year, we planned Shakespeare's *The Taming of the Shrew*. While *The Comedy of Errors* was pure farce, the *Shrew* was a comedy with quieter, more serious overtones. We reached a new high of 175 towns and cities in the state that year. *The Taming of the Shrew* proved to be the most successful, financially and artistically, of all the productions undertaken, and it was a satisfaction to know that nearly fifty-five thousand students in the state had seen two Shakespearean plays.

---

* Twenty-five cents would have been worth about fifty-six cents in 1964, and $4.50 in 2019.

She Stoops to Conquer by Oliver Goldsmith was selected for the spring tour, and the performing group agreed that it went more smoothly than those on any previous tour. The thorough preliminary job undertaken in other tours was paying off. Audience response was excellent, perhaps because *She Stoops to Conquer* was on the school curriculum, and perhaps, too, because students were becoming conditioned to a theatre-going experience.

By the end of our fifth tour, we realized we were in serious financial trouble. The Rockefeller Foundation had made the grant of thirty-five thousand dollars contingent upon the State Board's continued interest in the project. All that was needed to indicate this interest was sufficient funds to establish a Department of Speech and Drama, which would have put the Washington State Theatre's program on a permanent basis. When the governor's budget appeared, it precluded the possibility of this development. The excitement created by the letter from the Rockefeller Foundation giving us the grant to start the Washington State Theatre in 1936 was equalled in intensity only by the gloom that descended when we received its message of regret in 1939. It was clear the Washington State Theatre was doomed and the Playhouse threatened.

We realized that any future we could devise would be dependent on our own efforts, with the help of those associated with us. Collectively, we decided who should and would remain on the staff of the Playhouse, and who should seek employment elsewhere. Those who were selected knew they were accepting an immediate future of extreme austerity. But no one refused, and somehow we managed.

In January 1939, the Administrative Committee of the Washington State Theatre sent word to the sponsoring high schools of the state that the spring tour of *Julius Caesar* would have to be cancelled in all communities to avoid incurring further deficits, a figure that now stood at three thousand dollars (the Repertory Playhouse eventually managed to pay off this debt). The Washington State Theatre had failed financially, but its contribution to the young people of the state had fulfilled our most extravagant expectations. Over the years, many people would meet us and say, "I'll never forget the day you came to our school and I saw Shakespeare."

The Meaning of "Theatre"

This seems a good point to define the word "theatre." A building that contains a stage, an auditorium, and the necessary physical equipment to put on a show is not necessarily a theatre. A theatre is, first of all, a group of people, of artists, if you will—actors, scene and costume designers, lighting and construction technicians, musicians, and a director or directors—all dedicated to producing, honestly and beautifully, plays of merit.

When I went abroad, there were pitifully few such theatres in England or America. Today, on this continent, with the successful advent of regional theatres such as the one I was associated with—the Globe in Regina, Saskatchewan—this concept has begun to take hold. I believe these regional theatres, and not the commercial theatres in the larger centres, are developing the ensembles to create truly good theatre.

A commercial producer in America, heading for Broadway, usually selects a play not because it is good but because it will make money. He collects a group of actors, among them a star or stars (often movie actors or actresses, because their names are usually better known to the public and therefore have greater box office appeal); a director who has never seen most of the actors before and whose connection with the production frequently terminates on opening night; scene and costume designers; and a technician to light the play.

Before or during rehearsals, the play may be "doctored" by someone not at all familiar with the author or his intentions but who is supposed to know what Broadway likes. And if these changes are not enough, the "angel" gamblers who have backed the play see rehearsals and have a go at it too.

If such a mélange achieves success, it is sheer accident and, success or failure, the results are equally hard on the actor. If successful, he or she goes on and on, night after night, for months—even years—in deadly repetition, often in a part of no particular distinction. Great ability can scarcely survive such success, and for young talent, it is death. If, during a reasonably long run, some distinction of style and harmony of purpose is achieved as the result of the association of the component talents, instead of being conserved as an experienced and efficient unit for the purpose of establishing true theatre, the group is scattered in the inevitable search for further employment.

As Julius Bab says in an article in the *Encyclopedia of the Social Sciences*, "A theatre, in the true sense of the word, is a unity, at the core of which is the living community finding some vital part of itself reflected in the creations of the dramatist and actor." The living community meant for us the *total* living community, anybody and everybody who wanted to work in it in some capacity or be an audience. All kinds and conditions of people worked in our theatre, from the society matron who came to rehearsals in her limousine driven by a liveried chauffeur, to the little man selling papers at the Pike Street Market, who had no telephone and no address because he lived in Hooverville, the shantytown of the Depression.

We wanted our audiences to be composed of the total community too, which was one reason for keeping admission prices within the range of everybody's pocketbook. My husband frequently said, "People should be able to afford theatre." And when it was not possible for them to meet even this modest price of admission, we gave them tickets.

We believed in the creative capacity of those who came to the theatre to work, whether as actors or in any other function necessary to the running of a theatre, and we believed that it was an opportunity and an obligation to assist in developing this capacity to the point where it could be identified as talent.

One of the most crucial areas in the operation of our theatre was play selection. When you sell subscriptions, it is necessary to offer variety. Even the Canadian Stratford Festival theatre eventually realized it could not go on producing only Shakespeare. It had to include other and different kinds of plays to gain and hold the interest of its audiences.

The classics are classics by virtue of having qualities that have stood the test of time, but the fact that they are classics is sometimes seen as diminishing their popular appeal. It was our experience, however, that the classics always attracted the largest audiences to the Playhouse and did the best business. With few exceptions, we never had "standing room only" for even the most attractive modern comedy, but the opposite was regularly true for our productions of the classics.

Controversy was the keynote of the work of playwrights in the 1930s. Our first production that could definitely have been considered controversial was Paul Green's *In Abraham's Bosom*. It was applauded as a great play in Seattle, but would not, at that time, have been given a production in the South. Only when the theme of the play touches a live nerve of the living community does it become controversial, and it is commonplace that plays that are controversial in one period come to be accepted in another as great drama. Practically all of Ibsen's plays created controversy. *Ghosts*, for example, led to uproars and protests in London and New York when first produced because it dealt with the unmentionable subject of inherited syphilis.

In 1934, we did another potentially controversial play, Albert Bein's *Little Ol' Boy,* which dramatized the brutalization of "problem" youngsters brought into the jurisdiction of a reformatory. Our production of *Little Ol' Boy* got very favourable responses from the press and audience. Sermons were preached on it. Women's clubs, the Seattle PTA, even the mayor and his wife, participated on committees to promote the production. We received such recognition for doing a play that, however well or ill it might have fared at the box office, should have been produced.

Though Seattle audiences applauded plays exposing injustices in a Georgia turpentine camp or a Tennessee reformatory, we cut a little closer to the bone when we produced Eugene O'Neill's *The Hairy Ape*. O'Neill, more than any other single American, was giving a new life and a new significance to American theatre.

The play is laid in the days when stokers such as Yank fired ocean liners with coal. When the lady from first class insists on seeing the stokehole, she faints, frightened by the grease, dirt, and sweat of this great man. Paddy, one of Yank's shipmates, says, "She tought you was a great hairy ape, escaped from de zoo." This is a traumatic experience for Yank, who now believes he is not what he thinks he is, not even a man. Others see him as an animal, an ape, and he belongs nowhere.

One reviewer commented on a bit of Jack-created action when Yank receives his union card from the Industrial Workers of the World (IWW) secretary. "He holds it like a foreign thing for a moment in his great paw, then digs in his trouser pocket and says, 'Four bits? Is dat all?' It is one of the most heart-gripping, moving things I have ever seen in the theatre."

What Yank received for his fifty cents was a red membership card in the IWW, the "Wobblies," a name bestowed on it by a Chinese restaurateur who was unable to pronounce the abbreviation IWW. The IWW was attempting to organize the migratory workers, the "working stiffs" as they called themselves, into One Big Union. During the First World War, lumber prices soared astronomically but wages and working conditions remained unchanged. The Wobblies had no difficulty organizing, but when they called a strike in 1917, and ten thousand "working stiffs" downed tools and walked out of the camps, what sympathy they had from the general public evaporated. Someone said it was "more patriotic to kill a 'Wobbly' than a German." Anyone caught carrying a Wobbly card was in for a very tough time. So the red card in *The Hairy Ape* touched a live nerve in certain segments of the community. Everyone praised the production, but many criticized the play itself and the Playhouse for doing it. One of our own board members remarked, "It was a beautiful production, but aren't you afraid it'll give people ideas?"

The sprinkling of dissent over *The Hairy Ape* turned out to be a mere summer squall compared to the storm that broke over our heads when we produced Clifford Odets's one-act play, *Waiting for Lefty.* Even before the play opened, storm clouds began to gather around us. As the ticket sale was in the hands of a committee, tickets were not available at the theatre box office. This was standard practice: when groups took tickets for a performance or a block of seats, they sold them and only the unsold tickets were returned for box office sale. But in the case of *Waiting for Lefty,* gossip built this into some sort of conspiracy.

At the same time, several seemingly unrelated incidents were taking place that would eventually bring the roof down on our collective heads. As few people travelled to the Soviet Union in those days, I was asked to speak on my experiences there to any number of organizations and clubs—the Junior Chamber of Commerce, the Elks' Club, women's groups, and many others. Among the requests was one from the Unemployed Citizens' League. This group had organized the first self-help arrangements among the unemployed in the United States in the dark days of 1931. As I had not refused anyone who asked for my services as a speaker, I did not consider refusing to speak to them, even though I was warned that the audience might contain some political heretics and agitators. So, on a rainy night, I went to a gloomy hall on the skid road in downtown Seattle and spoke. When I talked about the theatre festival in Moscow, I got a bit of heckling about the political aspects, but I honestly told the hecklers I couldn't answer their questions because I didn't know anything about Russian politics.

Once before, after I had spoken about my trip at a large dinner attended by some members of our Playhouse board, one of them, a very nice man, put a friendly arm about my shoulders and said, "You make that speech too well. You're going to get people to like the Soviet Union." And that seemed to be a mistake, for it showed up in the furor over *Lefty,* with certain segments of the public drawing particularly dire conclusions from my speech to the Unemployed Citizens' League.

As well, that fall, we had rented our theatre to a church group whose minister had been asked to resign from a fashionable Seattle church because some of the more affluent members, who disagreed with him, were leaving the church and taking their support with them. What the issue involved was we neither knew nor cared. A committee from the breakaway church offered fifty dollars a month for the use of the theatre for Sunday morning services, an offer we accepted gratefully because we were having a real struggle just to meet current bills. When we began receiving telephone calls at the Playhouse complaining about the "Church of the People," as it was called, I went to a Sunday morning service to see and hear for myself. The minister was speaking on Abraham Lincoln, a seemingly safe topic, but, as a noted politician once said, "Mention Lincoln, but don't quote him." Our rental to this group, done quite innocently, later added fuel to the fire.

The production of *Waiting for Lefty* was a tremendous success. Many of the audience members had been out to dinner and arrived in evening clothes to immerse themselves in Odets's story of a taxicab strike, told sympathetically from the viewpoint of the strikers. It was an exciting experience for audience and performers alike, with great empathy developing as the play progressed. When the climactic cry, "What's the answer?" rang out from the stage, the audience responded, "Strike! Strike!" Al Ottenheimer wrote in his theatre log that night, "It was electric! The audience gave us five curtain calls and lingered in the theatre and in the lounge to discuss the show."

Since there was only one performance of *Waiting for Lefty,* and censorial effects accruing from it lasted for nearly a decade afterward, it is pertinent to note that, from those who actually attended, there was no protest. It is pertinent to note, too, how we who were involved in the production felt about the play. In the same log entry, Al admitted the bias of Odets's play but emphasized its solid artistic qualities:

> It has a message, a bitter tirade against racketeering in trade unions, and, likely, something of a Communistic bias, but the play transcends

> these. Its dramatic excellence, excitement, and power cause these other considerations to fade into the background. *Waiting for Lefty* admirably fulfills a quotation Brooks Atkinson adopted from one of his correspondents in a recent issue of the *New York Times,* to this effect: "The propaganda play ceases to be propaganda when it becomes good drama." The universality of the drama, emotion, [and] passion in *Lefty* makes all other considerations of small consequence.

The axe fell on us on January 15, three days after the play's Sunday performance. Al was making his usual rounds of the newspaper offices with Playhouse press releases and received a cool reception when he reached the *Seattle Times,* the city's most influential evening paper. Nothing could be accepted from the Repertory Playhouse, he was told, until he had talked with Carl Brazier, the managing editor. Brazier kept insisting the Church of the People had sold the tickets for *Lefty*. It hadn't, of course. It had had nothing to do with the production, and the minister himself was not even in the audience to see the play. When the newsman barked, "Don't give me a lot of theoretical stuff about your right to play any plays you want to," Al asked, "Is freedom of speech, of which the papers make so much, and freedom of the press, which they so vigorously defend, also 'a lot of theoretical stuff'?" He didn't get an answer.

As the capper, the newspaper executive charged that the most horrifying of all our crimes was that we had "incited people in evening clothes to riot." I gathered he felt that if I had incited the members of the Unemployed Citizens' League to riot (he had also reamed Al out because of my "political" speech to that group), it would have been bad, but when you incite people in evening clothes to riot, you are really climbing into revolution. And of course, in a way, I suppose he was right. When people in evening clothes demand change, you may get it.

The upshot was that for the next decade the Seattle Repertory Playhouse was never mentioned in the *Seattle Times*. When it was absolutely unavoidable for the paper to give a report on some recital or other event that happened to have taken place in our theatre, it was simply referred to as "a theatre at 41st and University Way."

As individuals, our names were not printed in the *Times* until the Washington branch of the House Un-American Activities Committee got into action. Then our names made headlines. When Burton died, no mention was made in his obituary of his ever having had any connection with the Playhouse. The whole thing had definite overtones of George Orwell's *1984*. The press, always very vocal in defending its own freedom of expression, knows exactly the pressures to apply when someone else chooses to exercise the same prerogative.

We received many letters about *Waiting for Lefty*, both for and against. A surprising number of the complaints came from people who said they would never support the Playhouse again. In checking our subscription lists, we found that few if any of them had ever been in our theatre, and none of them, as far as we could ascertain, had ever been subscribers. Some letters came from people who protested the production of a play whose name they didn't even know. But many more came from people who applauded our efforts, though most of those hadn't seen the play either.

Rumours circulated, charges were made, some of them openly, most of them whispered. Our board held a meeting to discuss the "lefty" eruption and arrived at the consensus that, though wholly unintentional, the circumstances surrounding the performance were open to misinterpretation. Al summed up the meeting in his log: "The Board has taken no stand on the matter of whether we do the new things in the theatre with a social aspect or not."

One well-meaning friend suggested we do things like *Little Lord Fauntleroy*, "because you can get away with things like that." Instead, in May 1936, we produced George Sklar and Paul Peters's *Stevedore* with the Negro Repertory group. Where the theme of *Waiting for Lefty* was racketeering leadership in trade unionism, the theme of *Stevedore* was the dock strike in New Orleans. Seattle was no stranger to waterfront problems or striking longshoremen, and Harry Bridges was building his International Longshore and Warehouse Union on the

Pacific coast into a force to be reckoned with. One might have supposed that a play about the struggle to break a strike and destroy a waterfront union would have had repercussions, but protests about *Stevedore* were comparatively mild. It may have been that, since the locale of *Stevedore* was New Orleans, it seemed remote from similar issues in Seattle.

How do you deal with a situation that involves you in controversy with your public, whether with "patriotic loyal Americans" who protest the production of *Waiting for Lefty*, or with moralistic patrons who denounce a production of Stefan Zweig's arrangement of Ben Jonson's *Volpone* or Dorothy Parker's *After Such Pleasures*?

Al once replied to a critic of one of the above persuasions:

> Only two things are taken into consideration when we choose a play. One: Is it significant for some phase of life and literature? Two: Will our audiences like it? *After Such Pleasures* was chosen because Dorothy Parker is one of the most representative and important figures of contemporary American literature. You may not agree, but that is the evaluation of the world's critics. We felt that this, plus the fact that we ourselves consider the sketches highly amusing, justified the production. Outspoken, yes—somewhat vulgar, yes. But so, plainly,

> are the phases of contemporary American life which she reports and holds up to the purgatory fire of ridicule.

I believe it is fatal to compromise your insights in order to acquiesce to the demands made on you. There is only one way to respond: state your case and hope the playgoer will acknowledge your integrity and arrive at an understanding of your standards. Otherwise, you will be producing plays written about nothing for nobody. It seems strange to me now to remember the difficulties we had over controversial plays that touched on moral issues. I am sure no one today would raise an eyebrow over Zweig's *Volpone* or Parker's *After Such Pleasures*, when the musical *Hair* presents actors in the nude and four-letter words creep into almost every playscript. Playwrights reflect their age, and time sorts the value of their contribution.

Seattle was a very union-minded town then, and several unions began buying blocks of seats, and then entire houses, for their members. These were for a variety of performances, not just the "controversial" plays. Progressive leadership in the unions began planning educational and cultural programs for their membership. When the head of the meat cutters' local wanted to buy a performance for his union, one of our board members, a banker's wife, protested.

"Why do meat cutters want to come to a theatre?"

"Why shouldn't they come to the theatre?" Burton replied. "They won't bring the entrails with them."

Her opposition to the whole idea was so strong she resigned.

Someone once said there must be a climate for the arts. We found the climate very favourable in Seattle and in Washington as a whole, I think, as the heritage of decades of struggle by dedicated, forward-looking, imaginative people to achieve a viable existence in their environment. The arts advance in such struggles. It is a precondition not only of artistic advance but of artistic survival.

It delighted us to see unions concerning themselves with our theatre. We wanted the theatre to be part of the living community. We were in the community—how could we not be of it as well? So we went on producing plays we thought all kinds and conditions of people in our growing city should see.

The Advent of War

As the 1930s drew to an end, the dark clouds of the Depression began to lift. People were getting jobs making armaments for the impending conflict we all knew was coming. Austerity in the James family, however, increased, for in 1938 I was fired from my teaching job on campus, after eight years in my position. The Drama Department called my dismissal "reorganization." We believed, however, that the director of the Drama Department, Glenn Hughes, hoped my dismissal would cripple us financially so we would have to leave Seattle and seek employment elsewhere. The move, however, backfired. Following my dismissal, Sophie Rosenstein and Wilbur Sparrow, two other teachers in the Drama Department, resigned, and the students staged a strike. The students were protesting the loss of their teachers, but they were also protesting the fact that they were required to act in the Studio Theatre on

University Way, a small building Hughes had renovated in 1932 when he failed to get the Playhouse.

The students objected that they were being typecast and were required to spend money they could not afford to provide their own costumes, for the plays done were mostly moderns. The slogan devised for the Studio Theatre stressed gaiety in the theatre, and the students' slogan for their strike was "It's Not Gay!" (I hasten to add the expression had a much different connotation in 1938 than it would have today!) It was a very successful strike, probably the first of its kind on any campus in the United States, for the board of regents ordered the Studio Theatre back on the campus.

In 1939, we opened a new and different phase of work in our theatre with the establishment of a production unit, the Lyric Theatre. In that season we produced Gioachino Rossini's *The Barber of Seville,* with a lovely young Japanese woman as Rosina. We also did a modern version of Johann Strauss's *Die Fledermaus,* for which I wrote the libretto, as well as Giuseppe Verdi's *La traviata,* with Jarmila Novotná and Richard Bonelli of the Metropolitan Opera in leading roles.

We were working, keeping the doors open, and looking toward the day when the blight of the Depression would lift and, with a group of talented, trained actors, we would be in a position to provide some security and to pay adequate, if not fabulous, salaries so they could make a life for themselves in the theatre. (We never paid salaries at the Playhouse until we were able to pay everybody the same amount, minimal though it was.) And, with our workshops, we were developing new, fresh, vigorous talents. What we never lost was a feeling of solidarity, of loyalty—not to us but to an idea, without which no organization can really survive. Once a member of our board said, "I wish I could get my staff to work for me the way your people work for you." I replied, "They aren't working for me. They're working for themselves."

At this time, of course, we were certainly aware of the lowering clouds of war, although the United States didn't become actively involved until 1941. A few years previously, we had made friends with a Japanese lady studying at Cornish and invited her for Thanksgiving dinner. At the dinner table that evening, we talked of the Sino-Japanese War. She said, "In Japan, we are very afraid that this war in China will escalate to the whole Pacific. The military are very ambitious. They want all of China, Singapore, Hawaii, the Philippines, and Australia." It sounded laughable, but we were aghast all the same.

"That would mean war with the US and Britain."

"Of course," the lady said. Had we never read the *Tanaka Memorial*? "It's the Japanese *Mein Kampf.*" We had not read or indeed ever heard of it, but had the State Department ever read it either?

We had built the theatre, survived the Depression, created the Washington State Theatre and the Negro

Repertory, survived the loss of those theatres, and also survived, however slenderly, the loss of our paying jobs. With the advent of war, we entered the busiest years of our lives.

One Sunday morning, I had been listening to the New York Philharmonic on the radio. I had to get to the Playhouse for my Sunday workshop, so I snapped it off and hurried to the streetcar. When I alighted, someone from the Playhouse met me with the news. "The Japanese have bombed Pearl Harbor. We are at war." It was December 7, 1941, the "day of infamy."

I was not surprised, remembering the Japanese lady's warning. And hadn't we been anticipating it, consciously, subconsciously, for months and years? We had protested the mountains of scrap iron being loaded for shipment to Japan. Seattle was tearing up its streetcar tracks, New York was tearing down its elevated railroads. Harry Bridges, president of the longshoremen's union, had said, "That scrap will come back to us some day in the bodies of American boys." When Dutch Harbor in the Aleutians was bombed, some GIs from the New York area warned, "Duck, you guys. Here comes the Sixth Avenue El!"

The next day, December 8, we were blacking out windows, shielding all exposed lights, and installing special lights and a warning system at the Playhouse in case of bombings. Everyone was convinced bombings were inevitable, for at that time it looked as though Seattle would be a prime target, with the Todd Dry Dock, Sand Point Naval Base, Bremerton shipyards, and Boeing all easily accessible to bombing raids.

Shortly after war was declared, the number of male members in our acting group was decimated, as men were drafted for the armed services. I frequently cast a play not knowing whether the men in the cast would finish either rehearsals or the run before receiving their "greetings from Uncle Sam."

Along with running the theatre, it wasn't too long before we were involved in all kinds of activities for the war effort. Our first concern was for the young people who were leaving us for the far corners of the earth. Anyone over eighteen who could pass the physical was away. We started a newsletter, the *Playhouse Communiqué*. It carried stories about what was happening back home, quotes from the reviews of the current show, news about marriages, births, and the addresses of their buddies elsewhere. Frequently, we would get a letter from someone saying, "I'm pushing out, but my buddy would like to be on the mailing list. He's been reading my newsletters, and he feels he knows you." When the war was over, some of the boys who demobilized in Seattle came to see us as friends, even if they'd never been there before. They looked on the Playhouse as home.

Every Christmas, we sent parcels to all of them, the items recommended, the weight and size just so.

A lieutenant colonel, who had once been on our board, said the only parcel he received from Seattle at Christmas was from the Repertory Playhouse. Sending our communiqués and preparing the packages for Christmas were two of the highlights for us in this grim period.

Once, the bread of hospitality we extended to GIs in our area came back to me as cake. During the war, I was on the Travelling Fellowship for the National Theatre Conference. I got off the train one rainy night in Austin, Texas, tired and hungry. It was wartime, the trains and hotels were very crowded, and if you missed a room reservation by even a short while, it was given away. My train was very late, and I knew my room must be long gone. As I stood there debating whether to spend the night in the railway station or in a hotel lobby, I heard my name called. A delegation was there to meet me. I was given supper and whisked away to spend a delightful three days as the house guest of a member of the university staff. When I expressed my gratitude, and some surprise, at their overwhelming courtesy to a total stranger, they replied, "Do you think we in Texas are less hospitable than you at the Playhouse in Seattle are to our GIs?"

During the war period, we were individually and collectively engaged in intensive activity, even with our depleted personnel. We did forty-nine performances for army camps and various service groups, nineteen special events, eleven Victory Square programs, sixty-eight radio programs, worked on War Chest campaigns, and sent out communiqués every month to eighty-four men and women in the armed services. All but the radio programs were done on a volunteer basis as our contribution to the war effort.

Doing the shows for the armed forces, the people from the theatre met some of these servicemen. As I never minded people watching rehearsals, it was not unusual to see men, Black and white, in the uniforms of the various services, sitting in the theatre at rehearsal, waiting for the actors to go out for coffee. They were, of course, invited to the cast parties. No person in uniform was ever refused a ticket, and comps for admission were available at the PXs (or post exchange, a store found on US military bases).

I began using men from the armed services who were stationed in or around Seattle. Several of them had had experience in theatres similar to ours and were pleased to get out of uniform and work with a theatre again. A couple of them turned out to be very good actors, relieving my casting problems a bit.

We had a memorable experience with a show we did to recruit workers to build the bombers at Boeing. The show was the responsibility of the military and was done in the university stadium. Bob Hope was master of ceremonies, and General Hap Arnold was the speaker. One of the high points of the show was a dramatized attack by GIs coming in from Lake Washington in assault boats, with a fleet of planes flying overhead. The floor of the stadium had been so thoroughly mined by an overenthusiastic dynamiter that when the mines went off, they blacked out more than a thousand lights. The mines were blanks, but the smoke was real. For a few minutes things were tense in the crowded stadium, but a light wind cleared the smoke and the show went on. It cost the army eight thousand dollars to put the stadium back in shape—but then, the military always has money.

A nice dramatic moment occurred at the show when Bob Hope said to the audience, more than ten thousand of them, "When the lights in the stadium go out, everybody strike a match." The lights were doused, the huge arena was in total darkness, and when the audience struck the matches, it lighted the entire area. "You see," said the master of ceremonies, "that's what can happen when people do something together."

With all this work for the war effort, we were still putting on our productions for adults and for our youth audiences. Christmas and Easter matinees were devoted to the children. For our adult audience at this time we did a most successful production of *Lady Precious Stream,* a translation of an old Chinese play by Xiong Shiyi. The play was done for China Relief, with the active interest of the Oriental Society and the Chinese community, who loaned us fabulous costumes for the play. Two Chinese actors, one an actor of male roles and Chin Shu Yin, an actor of female roles, directed the cast in the formalized techniques and manner of acting in the Chinese theatre.

In 1945, as it seemed the war was coming to an end, we wrote and produced a revue called *Here Comes Tomorrow*. With Dmitri Shostakovich's stirring song, "United Nations on the March," ringing in our ears, we dramatized our hopes for a united world, brotherhood, and peace. We felt we had had enough.

But that was not to be. Other forces were at work, preparing for the police actions and other undeclared wars that have haunted and tortured the people of the world until we look at each other and wonder if we are as civilized as we think we are.

We planned another musical in 1946. This was *San Juan Story*, based on the Pig War in the San Juan Islands. Just before the American Civil War, American farmers had become a thorn in the side of the British Hudson's Bay Company in the San Juans. The border in the San Juans had never been clearly defined, and when, one Fourth of July, the British saw the American flag flying over what is now Friday Harbor, they brought in the British marines to establish their territory. The British were sensitive about borders. They remembered 1812, when the Americans had decided they needed Canada.

While all this was going on, the Hudson's Bay factor's pig got into an American farmer's potato patch and the American shot the pig. The factor tried to arrest the farmer and bring him into British territory at Victoria for trial. However, with the dreadful conflict of civil war going on at the same time, the struggle between the American farmer and the Hudson's Bay factor on a remote island seemed very small potatoes indeed. The people on the island, left to their own devices, found they had more in common than they thought. The British bought produce from the Americans. The Americans hired an English teacher from Victoria. They invited each other to their national holiday celebrations, the Fourth of July and the Queen's birthday, and they made peace. Several years later, William I of Germany settled the boundary to the satisfaction of the British and Americans alike. The theme of our musical was "the people make the peace."

To our amazement, *San Juan Story* provoked controversy. After the demise of the Washington State Theatre, we had continued doing matinee performances for the city's high schools of any classic or play we thought might interest them. The Junior League was sponsoring this, and one day a committee from the league came to see us. It had been to the *Post-Intelligencer* with its promotional material and been told by someone at the paper that *San Juan Story* had fourteen subversive incidents in it!

The *Post-Intelligencer* had mentioned in particular the song that closed the show. This was "It's One World, Boys," sung by a double male quartet composed of the British marines and the American soldiers on guard at what was called the "marker tree." During the conflict, any British or American who dared put one foot over the line at the marker tree ran the danger of being shot. In the song, the boys sing of their homes in England and the United States, concluding with the double quartet singing "It's One World." The idea and the title for the song came from a book that Wendell Willkie had written, *One World*, based on his experiences during a trip around the world as a roving ambassador for President Roosevelt.

When Burton heard that the *Post-Intelligencer* wished to censor the script, he was adamant. "Not a line, not a comma, will be changed. The *Post-Intelligencer* doesn't censor our scripts." We played the show without incident, and I am certain no one was subverted by it.

When the war in Europe was ended and the Nazis defeated, we expected further conflict in the Pacific with the Japanese. But after the fearful bombing of Hiroshima and Nagasaki, the war was over, and the men started coming home. There had been casualties among friends, but none in our immediate group, and, to our great satisfaction, not a single mental casualty. Actors are often considered temperamental, perhaps even unstable, characters, but our actors survived the dangers and rigours of their various experiences very well.

Recreation for All

Once the war was over, the problems created and intensified by the war effort began to emerge. No state had been more changed by the war than Washington, whose population had grown by more than half a million as men and women flooded into industrial plants and shipyards. Migration prompted by military and industrial activity had profoundly disturbed established community life—assimilating thousands of strangers could not be accomplished painlessly in so short a time. Newcomer and resident alike were affected, and in some instances there was open hostility.

Winning the war had taken priority over everything else. Communities had had to mobilize for the emergency tasks of housing and integrating the new population into community life. Cities and towns, government and private organizations had girded themselves for the job. In the process of mobilizing their recreational resources, communities unified their forces and had an opportunity to observe the effectiveness of community-wide programs, bolstered by good leadership and adequate financial support. At the end of the war, these agencies began to wind up their affairs and terminate the recreational work. Federal funds were withdrawn and communities were left without the necessary finances and advisory help to maintain facilities and carry on adequate recreation programs. Yet the community problems created by the war did not disappear; they only became more acute.

Burton had toured the state of Washington in the 1930s and had been impressed with the interest and enthusiasm of many of the people he met for something comparable to our theatre to be developed in their communities. These people, sponsors of the tour for adults, were members of church groups, service clubs, and women's organizations. They talked of the needs their young people had for opportunities to engage in some kind of cultural programs in an organized way. Sports in school were usually organized, but everything needed more and better facilities. What they seemed to need most was leadership, perhaps some kind of central organization that could provide consultants to evaluate and coordinate activities, as well as indoor and outdoor recreational facilities.

Burton, remembering the needs, interests, and concerns of these communities before the war, and apprehensive that programs acquired during the war would be abandoned and the facilities fall into disuse and disrepair, asked for a grant from the state legislature of 1945 to conduct a recreational survey of the state. This forward-looking legislature appropriated the funds for what was to be called the Recreational and Cultural Survey of the State of Washington, begun in January 1946.

Technological advance (whereby machines took over more and more actual labour, a process accelerated by the war effort) and the increasing efficiency of the workers themselves had shortened the working hours of homemakers, factory workers, and farmers, giving all segments of society more leisure. But the very changes that had given more leisure had destroyed the base of traditional leisure activity. Spontaneous and informal neighbourhood life, formerly a major focus for leisure, had largely disappeared.

One of the strongest characteristics of pioneer days in the west was a sense of neighbourliness. People were short of funds, short of help, and short of equipment; hence, the natural tendency was to work together, to play together, and to make one's own amusement. Now composite schools were taking the place of the little red schoolhouse, which had provided the centre for culture and recreation for small towns and villages. As society became more settled and urbanized, common interests gave way to special interests. Instead of being participants in organized sports, people became spectators in stadiums.

The fieldwork on the survey was a tremendous task, and without the help of hundreds of people who spent thousands of hours of diligent, conscientious work, a task of such scope could not have been accomplished. Hundreds of conferences and community meetings were held in every part of the state. Findings and conclusions were referred to the people again and again for evaluation and comment, which served as a continual check on the work being done.

The survey found that, rather than constructive activities, what was emerging were undesirable leisure-time pursuits that could and did develop into problems. First, there were acute handicaps facing young people. These were especially complex for the children of migrant families, living in trailers and all sorts of temporary dwellings. Juvenile delinquency was soaring upward in all strata of society, marked by an increase in alcoholism and sexual promiscuity among teenagers. The story is far too familiar—truancy, school dropouts, vandalism, too much spending money, too little parental control and supervision, and too little community understanding and help. Young people felt isolated. The survey also found little or no provision was made in communities for adult and senior citizen groups, thus further dividing the common interests that integrate communities. Survey findings demonstrated that, on the whole, desires for unified programs for recreation were far ahead of any provision made to meet them.

The survey noted the effect the growing problem of pollution had on the recreational resources of the state. At that time, its chief concern was with water pollution. Atmospheric pollution from industries and pollution from insecticides had not yet emerged as threats. Water pollution was affecting large areas of river and lake recreation grounds, which were already shrinking through private ownership.

It was the survey's considered conclusion that communities should expect their needs to be met by state government, which should accept the fundamental responsibility of serving them in recreation as fully as it did in other fields. The committees that had given so much of their time to the work of the survey indicated their willingness to accept responsibility for their share of the work to follow, but they needed authority. They required funds and guidance, and these could only come from state involvement in the problem.

The concerns expressed by towns and cities in the state of Washington in 1946 have now become the concerns of the nation, indeed of the world, demanding solutions. The survey's report, *Recreation for All,* was presented to the 1947 legislature. But this legislature was in no mood for culture or recreation. It did not move on the survey, but it did set up the Un-American Activities Committee, with a budget of $158,000.

The Cactus

Robert Cromie, late editor of the *Vancouver Sun,* asked me how we were financed, and I told him of our problems and how we met them. He laughed and said, "Have you ever read Luther Burbank's *The Harvest of the Years*? I'm going to send you a copy so you can read the chapter on his work with cactus." The cactus, Burbank said, has adaptability. It seizes life, "adjusting itself to apparently impossible circumstances and doing the right thing at the right time and in the right direction." That was us, all right.

In twenty years, we had realized many of the objectives we had set for ourselves in our initial planning. We had developed an excellent theatre for the very young audience. We had created the Washington State Theatre for the high school groups. We had produced plays that had involved, either as audience or actual participants, members of every ethnic group in Seattle.

We had produced nineteen original scripts; we had toured the Northwest; we had produced with notable success the great classics—Shakespeare, Ibsen's *Peer Gynt*, and Goethe's *Faust*. We had developed a good school of theatre, which included actor and director training and all the skills necessary for the management of a theatre. We had created children's classes with a sound educational basis. We had made intensive contributions to the war effort, and we had done a survey of Washington that would enable another agency, some years later, to program leisure and recreational activities for the state.

Over the years, we had developed a philosophy that enabled us to meet exigencies and to turn them to our advantage. We had survived the loss of our building, the loss of jobs at the university, the loss of the subscription sales that had provided our working capital, and somehow managed to live and work. We met many difficult situations that eventually came to seem salutary, for they strengthened our will and determination and were as nothing when we were able to chalk up a victory—and we usually did just that.

When we failed, we would carefully consider the reason for failure and its extent. A failure can be a wonderful learning experience, sometimes teaching more than a success. Over the years, we constantly re-evaluated our business methods and studied the problems of acting and directing techniques, philosophically and artistically.

By 1940, our weekend workshops had developed into a full-time day school for students, mostly high school graduates who wanted to make theatre their profession. In 1944, the Junior Chamber of Commerce provided scholarships for high school graduates to attend our school. When the war was over, Congress enacted the GI Bill of Rights, which enabled returning servicemen to finish their education. Our school was accredited, and its activities were developed around a two-year course.

The men and women of the Playhouse were remarkable people. They worked well together, cementing friendships that have stood the test of time, or at least the test of forty-plus years. To them, the Playhouse was not just a place, a passing fancy, or a whim. It was something more, something that was integral to their lives, something they cared very deeply about, and worked incredibly hard for.

When, in 1936, the deepening pressures of the Depression closed in and the financial situation became even more acute, the working force of the Playhouse group seemed to be handed more and greater responsibilities by the board. The workers decided something in the nature of a guild was necessary and formed a group with a chairman and a set of rules or bylaws. This organization called itself the Organized Workers of the Seattle Repertory Playhouse, or OWSRP. It planned committees to assist in promotion and sales, and to determine policies and other matters of general importance to the group as a whole. It was decided that anyone who had actively worked in the Playhouse for a year in any capacity could apply for membership. This organization never outgrew its usefulness, and the democratic process at work stood the Playhouse in good stead during the war years and the darker years ahead.

Sir Tyrone Guthrie, in his autobiography, *A Life in the Theatre*, commented that a theatre, no matter what its glamour or level of subsidy, can be weak where it should not be weak: at the heart. We had created a theatre with a strong heart. We had developed "group communication" between people who were all intent on one purpose and, in achieving that purpose, had built cooperation in an extremely competitive area, the theatre, and in a culture whose dominant philosophy is competition.

We had some exciting experiences in those years when our theatre played host to travelling artists, particularly the folk singers—memorable evenings with Pete Seeger, Earl Robinson, and Woody Guthrie. One evening, Earl Robinson gave the first public performance of *The Lonesome Train*, the story of Abraham Lincoln's funeral train as it travelled from Washington, DC, to Springfield, Illinois.

One day, a battered old car, threatening collapse at every gasp of the engine, drove up to the Playhouse. A young man carrying a guitar stepped out, dressed in the attire embraced by the youth of today but not so usual then. It was Woody Guthrie. A performance was given for his benefit, and George Taverniti, who had an uncanny knowledge about cars and how to give even the saddest case a new lease on life, took over Woody's vehicle. Guthrie gave a most successful performance and came home with us afterward, sitting on the floor of our living room, repeating his repertoire into the early hours of the morning. Two songs I remember from that night so long ago were "Talking Union" and "This Land Is Your Land," which much later became a sort of theme song for young people in both the United States and Canada. Guthrie said, "My songs tell you something you already know." He told us he had bought his young son Arlo a guitar. His wife thought it too expensive for such a small boy, but Woody said, "We'll start him with the best and he can go on from that." When we planned our twentieth anniversary at the Playhouse, we wrote to our friends, asking them to sponsor the event. Guthrie wrote back, "I don't want to sponsor the Playhouse. I want to marry it."

On the evening of September 17, 1947, we opened the season of our twentieth anniversary. We received local and national recognition, telegrams and letters, and a particularly heartwarming message to the audience and to us from Helen Hayes, first lady of the theatre, live via magnified long-distance telephone from New York:

> Hello, Seattle!
>
> Hello, Burton James—and the Repertory Playhouse. This is Helen Hayes. I'm so glad to

be able to talk with you, especially at this time. I wanted you to know, at the very outset of your Twentieth Anniversary Season, how we feel about the Seattle Repertory Playhouse, and the wonderful work you're doing. . . .

To paraphrase Walt Whitman: "Great Audiences make Great Theatres." The Seattle Repertory Playhouse has helped to build the audiences which, in turn, have helped the development and growth of the theatre. . . .

I'm greeting you, not only for myself but for our national theatre organization, ANTA, the American National Theatre and Academy. When your kind of cooperation is extended, as it should be, between all the theatres, whether they're community, professional, or academic, then we'll begin to have a national theatre that will enrich the lives of all the people of our country. . . .

Our theatre is better, finer, fuller, because for twenty years, there in the farthest western reach of the United States, the Seattle Repertory Playhouse has been striving and struggling and pioneering and building. Our theatre is the richer for your effort. Our country is a better place to live, because of you.

Here's to the next twenty years—and HAPPY BIRTHDAY.

The next twenty years.

It seemed that night as though we could do the next twenty years standing on our heads after the way we'd persevered and come through the first twenty. But we were wrong about that. In 1948, not even twenty months later, the Un-American Activities Committees got into action. We were on our way out.

Convictions Held at an Agonizing Cost

In January 1947, our state legislature had set up the Joint Legislative Fact-finding Committee of the State of Washington to inquire into subversive activities in the state and report back to the 1949 legislature. State Senator Albert F. Canwell chaired the committee. This interim committee received the approval of the Washington Supreme Court, although by a divided opinion, and was in business.

The resolution setting up this fact-finding committee on un-American activities directed the committee to investigate all groups who "under cover of . . . the Bill of Rights seek . . . to destroy our liberties and our freedom by force, threats and sabotage, and to subject us to the domination of foreign powers." The resolution further directed the committee to investigate the activities of groups or organizations or educational institutions "supported in whole or in part by state funds . . . whose membership includes persons who are communists, or any other organization known or suspected to be dominated or controlled by a foreign power."

This madness hadn't sprung to life full-blown in the state of Washington, of course. It had been building and growing, fomenting in the frenzied situation that existed all over the country at that time. The Second World War had ended on May 8, 1945, when the German generals, in the presence of American, British, and Soviet generals, signed the terms of unconditional surrender. On September 2 that same year, the Japanese acknowledged defeat. Fascism was beaten. Hitler and Mussolini were dead. Though it had been costly, the Allies had achieved their victory.

Winston Churchill, at the time of the signing of the unconditional surrender of Germany, sent this message to Joseph Stalin: "Future generations will acknowledge their debt to the Red Army as unreservedly as we do who have lived to witness their proud achievements." During the conflict, on February 23, 1942, General Douglas MacArthur said, "The world situation at the present time indicates that the hopes of civilization rest on the worthy banners of the courageous Russian Army."

However, in spite of these tributes to the Soviet Union that recognized its contribution to our common struggle, it wasn't long before we were being urged to set up the same kind of situation that had created fascism, brought Hitler to power, and inevitably resulted in the Second World War. Not quite a year after his glowing message of thanks to Stalin, Winston Churchill mounted a platform beside President Truman in Fulton, Missouri, and called for an extension of the anti-Communist faction he had helped to construct after the First World War to meet "the growing challenge and peril to Christian civilization" of atheistic Bolshevism. In the halls of Congress and in the press, the call went out. The name of the game was "Let's get tough with Russia now." We had the atom bomb. What were we waiting for? The Soviet Union would not be able to make one for ten years. (As it turned out, it made one in three, which only added fuel to the anti-Communist crusade, by then in full swing.)

On January 3, 1945, at the opening session of the 79th Congress, Representative John E. Rankin, in a surprise legislative coup, put through a bill creating a permanent House Un-American Activities Committee under the nominal chairmanship of Representative J. Parnell Thomas. Thomas had been a member of the Un-American Committee, chaired by Representative Martin Dies, who, since August 1938, had carried on a ceaseless, virulent campaign against everything forward-looking and progressive in America, calling all such efforts Communist-motivated. The people engaged in these activities were labelled Communists, Communist dupes or fronts, and agents of a foreign power. Dies and his "sordid procedures" left the scene in 1944 when three members of his committee were defeated at the polls and Chairman Dies announced he would not run again.

With the advent of Rankin's House Un-American Activities Committee, state committees proliferated like poison mushrooms. Washington's Canwell Committee made headlines from the very beginning. The news media announced breathlessly that the first targets of investigation would be the Pension Union and the University of Washington. Shortly after the Supreme Court decision that approved the committee, the Washington Pension Union found itself under attack.

Some time earlier, the senior citizens of the state had organized themselves into an effective working union. They had persuaded the state to raise pensions from thirty to fifty dollars a month and to institute the first comprehensive health program in the nation, which enabled all pensioners to receive full medical and hospital care, including medicines and appliances, with freedom to select their own doctors. The Pension Union was also involved with other pressing issues of the time—more aid to schools, better social security, fair employment practices legislation, and better veterans' bonuses—and could always be counted on for strong support of any issue for the benefit of the state and the nation.

The Canwell Committee victories in the Pension Union hearings were small, although the legislature that set up the committee reduced pensions and deprived pensioners of the right to choose their own doctors. This first hearing by the Canwell Committee seemed to be a "try on." The committee then brought up its big guns to take on the University of Washington. Investigators began to prowl the campus. Intimidation (threats of subpoena, loss of jobs, and blacklisting) was freely used among the faculty to get individual professors to admit to membership in the Communist Party and to name others as radicals. The quality of teaching, writing, or research of professors was only lightly questioned. Instead, the investigators were intent on identifying those who were active in their union and in university affairs or had been active in any liberal, social, or political organization. Canwell announced in the press that there were 150 such subversives on the campus and that his committee would find out the facts about them.

The university administration forbade any public attack against the committee by the faculty, who were assured that members' rights would be protected but were told that nothing should be done to jeopardize the reputation of the university. This tactic, plus intimidation by the investigators, successfully kept the faculty divided, silent, and paralyzed, innocently hopeful that the whole thing would blow over. The University of Washington was the first educational institution in the country to give aid and comfort to an investigating committee. Assurances and protestations notwithstanding, on June 19, 1948, the committee delivered subpoenas to twenty-five or thirty professors and three members of the Playhouse staff, for hearings to begin on July 19, a time when faculty and students would be scattered and disorganized.

During the Pension Union hearings, no mention had been made about subversion at the Playhouse, which, of course, was not a part of the university at all. Our first intimation that we were to be involved came when we were rehearsing for our summer show, Charles MacArthur and Ben Hecht's *The Front Page*. As it was a newspaper story, we approached the Newspaper Guild to buy a block of tickets for one of the playing nights, and it asked for the opening performance. A short time later, we received a letter cancelling the arrangement. Al Ottenheimer called one of his friends in the guild and asked the reason for the cancellation. In the best cloak-and-dagger tradition, the friend asked Al not to come to his office but to meet him for coffee in a restaurant. There, Al was told the heat was to be taken off the university and the Playhouse was to become the committee's prime target.

At this time, the university was building a medical school, costing about six million dollars. The board of regents was worried it would be difficult to staff the new medical school if it were bruited about that the university was a hotbed of subversion. The man from the guild told Al that the regents had approached the committee with the request that it lay off the university.

As the university administration had been so agreeable and helpful to the committee, it was apparently not difficult to get Canwell's cooperation. Investigation of the university shifted into low gear and a new target had to be found to provide the same publicity.

It served no purpose for these small-time politicians to investigate some card-carrying Communist making speeches nightly on skid road. Canwell was more interested in getting publicity than in investigating subversion. He hungered to be a United States senator. Some inspired person or persons apparently chose this auspicious moment to point the finger at the Playhouse. We fit Canwell's requirements: we were "almost university," we were actors and therefore somewhat suspect to begin with in some minds, we had certainly been active in various union, university, liberal, social, and/or political affairs over the years, and we were newsworthy people whose faces and names were regularly seen in public.

So, one day in June, two men carrying handsome briefcases drove up to the Playhouse in a shiny car, armed with subpoenas for Burton, Al Ottenheimer, and myself. We were commanded to go to the "146th Field Artillery and remain there until discharged by the committee."

On the grim morning of June 19, 1948, we, along with forty other people, sat in a barracks-like room behind ropes, guarded by city and state highway police and some soldiers, to listen to "friendly witnesses" (friendly to the committee) brought in from all over the country. These witnesses were all professional anti-Communists: J.B. Matthews, former investigator for the Dies Committee, Howard Rushmore, a New York reporter for a Hearst newspaper, and George Hewitt, the sole witness against me, who said he had been a Communist for eighteen years and in the Soviet Union for two and a half years.

We listened to their shabby fabrications of crimes we might have been able to commit, had we had the opportunity, such as dynamiting the Seattle waterworks. It was an interesting comment on the characteristic thinking of these witnesses that they would think of dynamite, then a tool of construction, as a weapon of revolution, long before it became a later generation's symbol of protest.

Having been told it was most unwise to go before this committee without legal aid, we had hired a lawyer. Our lawyer, Cliff O'Brien, told us to answer no questions on our activities or beliefs, that the First Amendment of the Bill of Rights guaranteed freedom of belief and assembly. Or we might refuse to answer under the Fifth Amendment, guaranteeing the right to be silent, which protects the individual against self-incrimination. We chose to answer under the First Amendment, rather than the Fifth, for the words "self-incrimination" seemed to us to indicate guilt of some kind.

We, like many people, did not know the history of this amendment, so bitterly fought for by Thomas Jefferson and others to secure its inclusion in the Bill of Rights. The cogency of the Fifth Amendment was demonstrated at these hearings, for a university professor had invoked it and was therefore not indicted for contempt of the committee. It did not, however, save his university position—the board of regents dismissed him. (Ironically, the chairman of that board of regents, Dave Beck, boss of the teamsters' union, some years later was indicted for crimes that sent him to McNeil Penitentiary; he used the Fifth Amendment more than a hundred times during his defense.)

Witnesses friendly to the committee spoke without hindrance and with legislative immunity, telling scurrilous stories of crimes committed, or about to be committed, by the forty people subpoenaed by the committee. We sat behind ropes, guarded by police, and were not allowed to object or answer this ridiculous testimony. The papers carried the witnesses' tales with banner headlines such as "Playhouse Red Recruiting Centre."

When George Hewitt took the stand, he told the committee he had met me in the Soviet Union in 1933 (I was there in 1934) and had been told I was a guest of the Soviet Union and had been ordered by Stalin to start the cultural revolution in the Northwest, which led to my production of *Waiting for Lefty* in 1936. When I could take no more of this preposterous fairy story, I rose to demand that the man be cross-examined.

Albert Canwell's gavel hammered me into silence, while he shouted, "We'll have no Communist speeches at this hearing!" He ordered me out of the hearing. I tried to leave unassisted, but two policemen took my arms, and I was carried from the room. When my lawyer tried to speak in my defense, he was thrown out too.

Later, at the trials, when Canwell was questioned about lawyers at the hearings, he said, "Oh, half the Bar Association was there." Which may have been true, but at one time there was only one lawyer left *in* the hearings, while the rest were out in the corridors, having incurred Mr. Canwell's displeasure. The two policemen who hauled me out were very nice—they looked embarrassed, put me in an air-conditioned room, found me a chair, and said they hoped I'd be comfortable.

We charged Hewitt with perjury, proven by his own testimony, but before he could be served, he was off on a plane to the congressional hearings in Washington, DC, where he was to appear again and again as a responsible expert witness, at a tidy daily stipend.

For five days we sat at these hearings. Then they were over and we were dismissed, coming home to read the blazing headlines in the newspapers. Canwell had saved the state of Washington from the machinations of university professors, respectable citizens, and three Playhouse actors. No one need fear the domination of a foreign power any longer.

In our summer show, *The Front Page,* there was a line of dialogue when an irate editor, trying to train a rookie reporter in how to write a story, says, "How many times do I have to tell you nobody reads the second paragraph—all they read are the headlines!" Ironically, it was the same in our case. The public saw the headlines and skipped the paragraphs that might have cast some doubt upon our "guilt."

After the hearings, the mother of a friend called and asked me to spend some time at their cottage at Home Colony, thirty-five miles from Bremerton. She thought I needed a rest and said that if I was interested, her husband would pick me up that evening.

I had been there only a few days, unwinding and renewing my resources, when a lady from the store at the foot of the hill came to the cottage to say I was wanted for a very important long-distance call. The only telephone was on a counter in the store, so there was no privacy about the phone call, which was from my lawyer, telling me I had been indicted and had to be at the county jail before six that evening. He told me I was out on five hundred dollars' bail, but not to worry because somebody had put up a property bond. However, I had to be at the jail before 6:00 p.m. or the police would come for me. I explained I was thirty-five miles from Bremerton, had no car, would have to take an hour's trip on the ferry—and would probably have to wait for the bus in the morning to get to Seattle from there. Before I got back up the hill to the cottage, three cars drove into the yard, offering to take me to Bremerton or wherever else I wanted to go.

I was at the county jail by nine o'clock the next morning, under my own steam and the steam of my friends, to be fingerprinted, mugged, and numbered. I can't remember the number they gave me. I should, I suppose, for not many people in my position, in that day, had that experience.

I didn't know who had put up the bond for my bail, but I was out and had to wait for the trial dates in the fall. The six people who had been indicted were a mixed lot. There were two university professors, a health officer who had reported unsanitary conditions in the kitchens of a swank Seattle club—he had been cleared by the Civil Service Commission in order to get his job and had taken the loyalty oath, but that didn't seem to count for much now—Al Ottenheimer, my husband, and myself. The charge was gross misdemeanour, "contempt of the state Un-American Activities Committee for willful refusal to answer a proper and material question," which was what Canwell laughingly called "the sixty-four-dollar question": "Are you now or have you ever been a member of the Communist Party?"

Before the trial dates were set, prosecuting attorney Lloyd Sharett called our lawyer and said if we would come down and plead guilty and pay a twenty-five-dollar fine, we would be spared the ignominy of trials. We were in no mood for that kind of cooperation with this contemptible committee. We had been given no opportunity anywhere to answer the lies told about us by paid witnesses and headlined so luridly in the press.

We felt our only recourse lay in challenging the legality of the committee and its procedures in the courts. So, with greater confidence in the courts than our later experience warranted, we told the prosecuting attorney what he could do with his "guilty" pleas and went to trial.

What had we and the Playhouse done to merit this attention from Canwell's committee? We had produced all kinds of plays, some controversial, that "gave people ideas," in the words of our board member who had resigned after *Stevedore*. We had signed petitions for senior citizens' pensions. We had actively participated in the war effort. We had protested the sale of scrap iron to Japan and concerned ourselves with the war in Spain. I had made speeches. We had created the Washington State Theatre and had helped conduct the Recreational and Cultural Survey of the State of Washington. At Burton's trial, the survey was the sole charge against him.

Canwell stated on the stand that he "had information" that Burton had siphoned money from the cultural survey project to the Communist Party. The newspapers carried the headline, "James Siphoned State Funds to Reds." At the time, a helpful if somewhat dim prosecutor asked, "But didn't James turn over ten thousand dollars back to the state from that project?" He was squelched and the papers did not carry that story.

In point of fact, none of those funds could possibly have been used for any purpose other than that for which they were intended, for every penny expended had to go through the secretary of state's office on vouchers. And it was all accounted for. The legislature that had provided funds for the survey, not trusting an actor to do an adequate accounting job, had appointed a legislator, with a salary and an expense sheet, to watch over the operation. He had to come to Seattle from out of town to do the job. At one point, he complained to Secretary of State Belle Reeves, "I'm supposed to be watching James, but *he's* watching *me*. You should see the way he combs my expense sheet. I'm damned tired of it!" Yet that man's accounting, and the vouchers supporting the accounting, were never brought forward as evidence.

Before our trials began, some uneasiness started to appear in the prosecuting circles. Prosecuting attorney Sharett asserted this was "a proper avenue of inquiry for the Un-American Activities Committee under the legislative resolution creating that Committee. Many serious questions of law will doubtless be raised as to the right to prosecute a person for contempt of a legislative committee." However, as defense attorney John Caughlan argued in Judge Clay Allen's court on October 4, 1948, "there is not any authority in the United States that gives any government body the right to inquire into what even a non-citizen thinks—either religious or political. These defendants are all lifetime American citizens."

Judge Allen took a week to search the law and his conscience, and found nothing that pointed to the Bill of Rights: "It is the court's view that committees created by the legislature cannot be expected to observe the same exactitude and accuracy in conducting their operations as would be expected of a court of law."

Our hopes rose at this hint that a court of law would act with "exactitude and accuracy." Perhaps we had been right in accepting this ordeal, for had not Thomas Jefferson laid down guidelines: "It behooves every man who values liberty of conscience for himself to resist invasions of it in the case of others; or their case may, by a change of circumstances, become his own. It behooves him, too, in his own case, to give no example of concession, betraying the common right of independent opinion, by answering questions of faith, which the laws have left between God and himself."

The trials began in October 1948. Dr. Herbert J. Phillips, from the Philosophy Department of the university, was the first to come to trial and was acquitted because of what the jury stated it considered "the elements of high-handedness of the Canwell Committee" and "the improper service of the subpoena by an interested party." Mr. Stith, the subpoena server and one of the investigators on the committee, was indeed interested in the extent of his six-thousand-dollar-a-year job, and the jury believed he had a "very deep feeling" against Dr. Phillips.

Next on the docket was the case of Dr. Ralph Gundlach, in the Psychology Department at the university. The prosecutor had taken pains to detach the affidavit of services from his subpoena, so the jury would not be able to consider that as a reason for bringing in an acquittal. Dr. Gundlach's case ended in a conviction.

As case after case came up for trial, the avenues for defense became more limited, until finally the judge's sole instruction to the jury as to grounds for conviction was "willful refusal to answer proper and material questions." The provisions for safety guaranteed by the Constitution and the Bill of Rights became, as Abraham Lincoln once said, "as thin as the homeopathic soup that was made by boiling the shadow of a pigeon that had been starved to death." Any attempt to question the legality and procedures of the committee was dismissed by the judge—"The virtue of this Committee has been established."

Again and again, on the stand, Mr. Canwell would say he "had information" on this or that. Finally, during my first trial, we asked that this "information"—files, cards, letters, whatever it was—be subpoenaed so the court could judge the validity of the material. If such information had existed, we could have been taking a daring chance in demanding it. We needn't have worried. Our action was dismissed as not material and Mr. Caughlan was put in contempt of court in the presence of the jury for his insistence that it be forthcoming, if indeed it existed.

Watching a jury being picked for a trial in which one is to be involved as a defendant is, to say the least, a learning experience. Watching the faces of the prospective jurors, hearing the questions asked by the lawyers and the judge, noting the answers, learning the jargon of the court provides intensive education. The defense and prosecutors were allowed three challenges to the jury panel when it had been selected. In the recess, both sides scanned the panel to discover if these individuals could bring to the trial the same objectivity and willingness to listen to evidence that they had declared, under oath, they were prepared to do.

During my first trial, a gentleman answered "none" when asked if he knew any reason why he should not be on the jury. He had been out of town during the hearings, and, outside of the fact that he had his own business to attend to, he could serve. He also mentioned he represented the United Fruit Company. We seriously questioned the objectivity of this man because of his position with United Fruit. We felt big business might not be sympathetic to our side of the issues. But as we scanned the panel, there seemed little choice. The other jurors all seemed to be in the same class. Thank God he made it to the trial. He hung the jury. He said he didn't know what this was all about, but he didn't like it. The high-handedness of the court proceedings disturbed him, and he would not bring in a guilty verdict on the basis of what he had seen and heard.

The jury had deliberated for twenty-nine hours, with the judge returning periodically to give instructions. The juries in the other cases had been out for as little as half an hour. It was all very heartening, but it meant I had to be tried again.

At my second trial, in July 1949, we became convinced there had been some serious mishandling in the selection of the jury panels. My defense did a thorough job and discovered the panels did not represent a cross-section of the community, as was the law, but had been weighted in favour of the more affluent sections of the city. Mr. Caughlan declared, "A series of grave crimes have been committed in the selection of the jury panels in King County," and he demanded a full investigation by all King County Superior Court judges. "This panel has been co-opted and disturbed," he said. "The names appear to be in proper order, but someone has altered jury district designations behind the jurors' names. All of this constitutes a violation of almost every section of the criminal code."

We demanded a grand jury investigation. The prosecution said they saw no need for that, and our action was dismissed. Stunned by judicial complacence in the face of such a serious charge, Mr. Caughlan protested, "I'm not quite sure Your Honour understands." The press reported that Judge D.A. McDonald's smile was indulgent: "I didn't come to town on a load of hay," he said, and carried on.

The trial proceeded in the pattern of the cases that had preceded it. Any attempt to bring in witnesses or testimony about my life and many years of work in the community was ignored or suppressed by objections from the prosecution and sustained by the judge, who sometimes rapped a tattoo on his desk to remind them to get into action.

The prosecution had brought in a female attorney for this trial, perhaps in an attempt to glamourize the proceedings—a woman trying a woman. She was no better and no worse than the men. No photographs were permitted in the courtroom during the trials, so the newspapers were reduced to trying for posed shots after court had recessed for the day. One man asked me if I would get back up on the stand so he could photograph the lady lawyer questioning me. I declined, as I thought we could do without that touch of glamour in any publicity for Canwell.

The verdict was guilty as charged.

The day this decision came from the court, our neighbour, a retired naval officer, called me and asked what had happened. When I told him, he gasped, "My God, I don't know what's happening to this country!" I must confess I had the same thoughts myself.

Finally, on the morning of July 19, 1949, I stood in the courtroom facing Judge McDonald as he prepared to pass sentence on me: "Mrs. James, a jury of this county has convicted you of the crime of willful refusal to answer a proper and material question before a legislative committee. What, if anything, have you to say why judgment should not be pronounced upon you?"

Earlier that morning, as my attorney drove me to court to be sentenced, he asked me what I was going to say when I was asked that question.

"I'm not going to tell you."

"You know they could charge you with contempt."

I was touched but amused. "After two trials, with what I've already endured, have I anything more to fear?"

It is court procedure at the conclusion of a trial to allow the prosecution and defense time for what is called a "summing up." I had asked my attorney to let me have a little of that time to talk to the jury, to let me get past all the legalisms that had so far obstructed my defense. He refused, afraid I might say something to spoil my case. But the time to answer the judge's question was to be all mine. As the old-timers would have said, I was gunning for bear that morning. After two trials in this court, the April one ending in a hung jury after twenty-nine hours of deliberation, and the one in July that ended in my conviction, I spoke from the depths of my being:

> Your Honour, I am at this moment in a strange and terrible position, not for any crime committed by me, for in fact, myself and my attorney were the only innocent principals in this action. I am about to be sentenced for a crime of which I have been convicted by a criminally selected jury. Irrefutable evidence of this crime was presented to this court. My action

in this cause was denied and no action whatever has been taken on this matter of criminally packing juries in these courts.

I accuse the court of denying me my proper defense, refusing permission for my witnesses to appear for me. Even my own daughter was refused an opportunity to appear in my defense on some flimsy legal pretext. The prosecutor has been given every opportunity for his witnesses, even including the testimony from one George Hewitt, who is now under indictment in his office for perjury. I accuse the prosecutor of defacing and destroying evidence—evidence so important in this action that in the first of these trials it won acquittal. Never once in the course of these trials have we been able to wring from these gentlemen that such evidence existed until the deputy prosecutor, John Vogel, was put on the stand, where under oath he impudently and brashly admitted that he himself had been guilty of this crime of removing, defacing, or destroying evidence. Now, finally—and this is so terrible I find it difficult to phrase the words—I accuse this court, you, Your Honour, of being biased and prejudiced against me, of giving every assistance within the power of your high office to the prosecution, and of

> being more concerned with obtaining a guilty verdict than with serving the ends of justice in this court.
>
> I feel in making this statement I am acting not only in my best interests but in the interests of every citizen who may find himself involved in the Superior Courts of King County.

When I finished speaking, the court was silent. The steno-typist asked my daughter for a copy of my statement, as he had failed to get it down.

The judge answered:

> I regret very much that you feel that way toward me. I never had any enmity against you or your counsel. There is no question at the time this Canwell Committee was launched that you were quite within your rights to oppose it. In fact, I might say that a great many members of the Bar, and indeed many judges, doubted the constitutionality of this, in fact, some of the Supreme Court judges.
>
> But of course, I am by my oath required to follow what the Supreme Court says, and before this hearing, the case which has generally been construed—which I believe was decided in April . . . March 18, 1948—the

case of the State ex. rel. Robinson v. Fluent held . . . it is true by a divided court, but I am bound by what the majority say . . .

The concurrent resolution of the 1947 legislature, which created the interim committee on Un-American Activities, was an authorized act of the legislative body, and it is effective for the purpose for which it was adopted. By that resolution, the legislature provided, as it had the inherent power to provide, for the payment of expenses of the members of the committee.

That has been taken by my colleagues and the Bar generally to have foreclosed the position you took. I want to say this for you. You have been consistent. Your real defense was that this committee was unconstitutional. Your counsel, I felt, realizing that the jury under my instructions could not very well have returned any other verdict than they did, attempted to show—which undoubtedly was true—that you suffered very great financial reverses by the actions of this committee. I have been accused of following a program—I believe that was the word—a procedure of other judges.

This is to your credit. You stood by your guns. You didn't commit any perjury. And maybe I am a little chivalrous, but I am not

> going to sentence you to jail. I don't regard you as a criminal in the ordinary sense, but I do think the jury had to find you guilty as they did. It will be the sentence of this court that you pay a fine of $125, and thirty days in the county jail, which will be suspended.

So there I stood, in an American courtroom, convicted of the crime of being consistent. After reading accounts of trials on similar issues held in later years, I realize I got off very lightly. Our trials in 1949 seemed to be a sensible expression of our court system when compared to the circus of the Chicago trials in 1969. Five of the six of us were convicted, with fines and jail sentences of thirty days for the men, a suspended sentence and a fine for me.

During the trials, Burton suffered a slight stroke. It was nightmarish, happening on top of our other tribulations, but Burton retained his spirit. It was after the stroke that Burton was sentenced. When his doctor heard he was to be jailed, he said, "My God, man. You can't go to jail. It would be fatal!" The sheriff told the prosecutor, "You're not going to put James in my jail. We'll put him in the hospital and hire deputies to watch him."

The court ordered a thorough physical examination. Burton was in the clinic for two days, at a cost of fifty dollars a day, which for some reason we did not have to pay—we seemed to have had to pay for everything else. The doctor's prognosis was that a jail sentence might be fatal, which could result in most unfavourable publicity. The court decided not to jail him but to put him on probation for a year. It then became necessary for Burton to report in person to a parole officer every thirty days. It was degrading and inconvenient, but life had to go on somehow.

That year of 1948–49 had been an incredible one. We had experienced the hearings, the long drawn-out trials, then the Court of Appeals, the State Supreme Court, and finally the United States Supreme Court, with divided opinions, all upholding the convictions. For weeks and months, we had lived literally on sheer nerves, with moments when we wavered on the brink of abject misery. Then a gradual awareness began to take over, and our lives gained some sort of equilibrium again. This awareness grew from our conviction that it was necessary and right that we should face this obscenity, not solely for ourselves but for the America that had given us life, liberty, and possible opportunities for the pursuit of happiness. We succeeded in holding firm to our convictions, but at an agonizing cost.

The judge's statement that I had suffered serious financial loss was quite correct. The theatre is particularly vulnerable to attack. It is a very public occupation, for it must successfully bid for public support to survive. Our incomes and those of our staff were dependent on the sale of tickets to our plays, income from the school, and periodic rentals. We had no assistance grants or subsidies. It was inevitable that, with the hearings and lengthy trials, some of those who supported the work of the theatre would react unfavourably. Surprisingly enough, both the theatre and we managed to survive—for a while, at any rate.

We produced our plays for the adult and children audiences and maintained the work of our schools. But in the summer of 1949, the most formidable blow of all fell. Burton was away, teaching in Banff, Alberta, for the summer when two men came to our theatre. They said they were from the Building and Grounds Department of the university and asked if they could look at the interior of the Playhouse. When they seemed to be going into every nook and cranny, I asked what their interest was. "The university is thinking of buying this place for the Drama Department," they said. Then they complimented me on the excellent condition of the building.

We were operating on a lease from Mr. Fitz, the owner. He had never mentioned any possible sale and had been most sympathetic during the turmoil of the Canwell business. I asked the men if Mr. Fitz had offered the theatre for sale. "He's a little reluctant, but we can condemn it if he proves too difficult."

An ordinance that enabled educational institutions to condemn property for their purposes had been enacted a year or so previously. With a very good cash offer for the property, and the prospect of condemnation hanging over him, Mr. Fitz did indeed agree to sell. Our lease ran until December 31, 1950. On December 30, the final curtain came down on George Bernard Shaw's *Pygmalion*, the last production at the Seattle Repertory Playhouse under our direction.

In January 1951, we moved our personal belongings to be stored in the building we had rented some years before for the Washington State Theatre. Our files, scripts, press books, and some pictures were sent to the University of Washington archives. A carload of flats, curtains, and trunks of costumes and wigs went to the Banff School of Fine Arts in Alberta. The university paid us thirty-five hundred dollars for the installations and other property we owned in the building. We paid all bills due, and with this money closed our theatre owing nobody anything. After twenty-eight years, our life in the theatre in Seattle was over.

There were some victories from the ashes. Canwell never did achieve his heart's desire. He was defeated in two primaries in his attempt to become a United States senator. His committee was defunct, and two or three of its members were beaten in the next election, including the legislator who had sponsored the bill through the 1948 legislature.

Much later, in 1955, I was even able to find some wry amusement stemming from the incident. At the conclusion of the trials and hearings, all records of the proceedings—including, I assume, the "information"

Canwell repeatedly referred to in the course of the trials, material we had tried so hard to have subpoenaed for review by the court and for which Mr. Caughlan, for his efforts in that direction, had received a contempt of court charge—were supposedly placed in three safes in a locked room at the legislative buildings. The legislature decided, in 1955, to turn this material over to the Federal Bureau of Investigation. Speaker of the House John L. O'Brien, Lieutenant-Governor E.T. Anderson, and an FBI agent unlocked the door of the room and had to drill open the safes—somebody had lost the combinations.

They found some dusty paper, Communist literature, and a history of the Soviet Union for beginners, but no records of either hearings or trials. Apparently, the elaborate efforts to protect these records were a huge joke. Canwell, when questioned, said he had burned the records at his home to keep them from falling into the hands of the Democrats and refused to say what he had done with the microfilm that had been made of this "controversial" material. Speaker O'Brien wanted Canwell placed in contempt of the legislature for refusing to answer proper and material questions. As O'Brien said, those records and documents "constituted property of the State and not of Albert F. Canwell, and the State didn't spend nearly $158,000 for Canwell's benefit." State Attorney General Don Eastvold and other Republican confrères saved Canwell the ignominy of an investigation.

We had other, more positive, victories. We became aware of the goodness of our neighbours, friends, and even total strangers: the people who had put up the property bond for our bail; the man, totally unknown to me, who paused a moment before me on the street and raised his hat; another man who came to the house one Sunday morning and apologetically handed me a twenty-dollar bill. "My wife and I think you might be needing money." (We did, for the six cases for the three of us from the Playhouse cost nearly twelve thousand dollars.) When I offered a receipt, he shook his head. "I'd lose my job if anybody knew I gave you money." Guilt by association.

The man in the tavern. It was late Saturday afternoon, and my daughter and I were in the courtroom waiting for my hung jury. I wanted a cup of tea. All the restaurants in the neighbourhood were closed, so we went across the street to a tavern for a glass of sherry. We sat at the counter, and finally my daughter said, "Mother, finish that. The man is filling your glass every time you take a sip." When I came to pay for it, he said, "It's on the house, lady."

One day, during the trials, I was standing waiting for a streetcar. An elderly lady standing near me asked if I would read the number on an approaching car for her. Then she peered more closely at me and asked, "Are you Mrs. James?"

"Yes, I am."

"Well, I want to shake your hand. I am a member of the Daughters of the American Revolution, and you are fighting for the very things my ancestors fought for." Then, as she mounted the steps of the streetcar, she turned back and smiled at me. "I wish you luck. It's a long battle, isn't it?"

All those blessed people. And the Playhouse board members, actors, technicians, members of the ethnic groups, Black and white and other colours, over fourteen hundred of them. Neither Canwell nor the prosecutor was able to enlist even one of them as a "friendly witness" for the hearings or the trials, and it wasn't because they didn't try. Particularly if they were immediately involved with us in any way, many of the group were pressured by their families and hounded by the FBI at their businesses or at their jobs.

The feeling of intense loyalty to the theatre was clearly revealed in the story of a young actress, told to me by her mother. She was a doctor's daughter, and one evening passed a Canwell investigator as she was leaving her father's office. He asked where she was going in such a hurry.

"To a rehearsal," she answered. "At the Playhouse."

"The Playhouse? Isn't that place shut down?"

She turned on him savagely. "No! Did you think you and that committee could shut us down? Think again!"

As she stormed out of the office, the investigator shook his head. "I don't understand it. They're all like that."

Sir Tyrone Guthrie, in his autobiography, notes the cohesive solidarity that can develop in a permanent acting company and is absent in the more casual and brief contacts in the profession. There may be personality gaps between individuals, but let the institution come under attack and they unite to rend the attacker. We had developed a real ensemble, without which no theatre can ever achieve great distinction. We should have been permitted a longer life.

I wish I could report that all the activity recorded in this chapter was unique, or a lone incident, but you know it wasn't. It was simply a small flurry, one of many over the years, in the struggle of some to maintain the democratic process in the United States. John Adams, second president of the United States, had a personal animus toward democracy and once said, "Remember, democracy never lasts long. It soon wastes, exhausts, and murders itself. There never was a democracy yet that did not commit suicide."*

It frightens me sometimes to see indications that Adams may have been right, that this great country really does have a self-destructive impulse. For example, a few years after our ordeal, we witnessed the advent of that noxious character Senator Joe McCarthy, who charged everyone, including Presidents Truman and

* "From John Adams to John Taylor, 17 December 1814," ***Founders Online***, National Archives, http://founders.archives.gov/documents/Adams/99-02-02-6371.

Eisenhower, with being "soft on Communism." And, at the time I wrote this, the media was labelling every protest march as Communist-led or -inspired, a shabby attempt to avoid confronting real problems that answers nothing and has never solved anything.

But this memoir is the story of a theatre and the lives of the people who created it and worked in it. Our charming building, with some nice modernization by the university, still stands at the corner of 41st and University Way in Seattle and is being successfully used by the Drama Department of the university for a generation of students who have never heard of us, or of the hearings and the trials.

University Way has changed considerably. Where in our day there was a dreary cleaning establishment, a small grocery store, and a gas station are now substantial office and bank buildings and, next to the bank, a very nice continental restaurant. One October day in 1969, I sat at a window of that restaurant, looking down and across at the theatre, and remembered that it was forty years before, almost to the day, that we opened the Playhouse with George Bernard Shaw's *Major Barbara*.

As a footnote to this chapter, I suppose I should put down, at last, the answer to the question that so many of our friends have wanted to ask over the years but have been too shy or polite to ask: No, we were not then, nor had we ever been. But, somehow, it didn't really make much difference, did it?

A Broken Heart

I never really meant to write a book. If things had turned out differently, this would have been Burton's book. But there were "portents," as it says in Stephen Vincent Benét's *John Brown's Body*, which made that impossible. And so, these many years later, I have tried to sit down and sift through the memories and memorabilia of a lifetime, to get it all down on paper, however imperfectly, for those who remember any part of those times now gone, and for those who are yet to come.

During the time of the hearings and trials, when Burton was teaching summer classes at the Banff School of Fine Arts in Alberta, the head of the school said to him, "Burton, when this is over, come to Canada. Come to Banff. I'm planning bigger and better things for the school, and you can be helpful." To the eternal credit of the Banff School and its administrators, no action or censure was ever taken against Burton there after the hearings, or indeed after his trial and conviction, nor did they allow anyone else to harass him or take action against him while he was there, though I understand the FBI made at least one attempt.

So we taught in Banff that summer, after the Playhouse ceased to exist. Following our stint at the Banff School, we went to Saskatchewan to teach a two-week workshop in drama for the Saskatchewan Arts Board, the second such visit we had made. The board was giving classes for community people, and the prospects for growth and development were very exciting. But even with prospects ahead, the strain and trouble had taken their toll.

During that summer, I could see Burton was failing fast. One day, after we returned home, I went to Burton's doctor and pleaded, "What should we be doing that we're not doing?" He looked away from me for a long time before he spoke. "I don't know," he said at last. And then, softly, "Did you ever hear of someone dying of a broken heart?"

My husband died on November 13, 1951. Someone remarked at the time that November 13, 1951, was the date of the opening of the first University of Washington production in our former theatre.

All Beginnings Come to an End

My husband's bright beginnings came to an end with the loss of his theatre. His death in 1951 was really just the final extension of that end. But his ideas and his influence still go on, I know, through the thousands of students he worked with, the thousands of people who saw him perform, spoke to him, met him, were touched by him, and through his daughter and her children, and now their children.

My life went on. I was blessed by new friends, who made a place for me in their lives, and by a happy quirk of fate that enabled me to keep working in the theatre long past the age when I might reasonably have expected to be put out to pasture. I have had many good and happy years in Canada, first with the Saskatchewan Arts Board and then with Globe Theatre, building a climate for theatre in the province and in my adopted country.

When someone talks or writes of a life full of memories of experiences lived to the full in growing up and growing old, reviewing the past might seem a trifle tedious. But remembering so much of yesterday's work, and the struggles in which we were involved, those memories seem as contemporary as today's headlines. All the problems we saw emerging nearly fifty years ago have reached a climax today. Then we thought that time and hard work would obviate the difficulties, but now time is of the essence. Will there be time before global disaster, from war or pollution, overtakes us, or will the future be silence? We don't know. The trouble with life today is the future is not what it used to be—the future is now, and it doesn't seem to be working.

Rusty Schweickart, the American astronaut, speaking in Saskatoon in the spring of 1971 during Earth Awareness Week, said, "Unless we solve the problems of this planet, that we viewed from space and which we were able to blot out with our thumb held at arm's length, it will be whirling through space as dead as the moon . . . and there isn't much time. Earth has the same limitations as a space ship, and no back-up systems as we had. If we blow it here, there's no other place to go."

I mentioned in my second chapter the inheritances and environmental pressures that guided me into the pattern that became a way of life. My inheritance gave me excellent health and lots of energy, and my environment gave me standards that have served me all my life—courage when courage was needed, and a determination to carry through with any project, no matter how difficult or frustrating, to complete what was begun.

Looking back from the vantage point of more than eighty years, I would have to say there's been more good than bad. My marriage could well have been described with that phrase from the fairy tales, "and they lived happily ever after." We always had the spiritual and physical stamina to stand up, lend a hand, and go on.

I remember the wonderful Black people who worked with us in the Federal Theatre Project on WPA, where I came to know the dedication they brought to something they thought important and rewarding, and we grew to understand and love each other. The project was set up to answer an emergency of the devastating Depression. If only an enlightened government had seen fit to develop a national arts project with representation in the Cabinet, what a different story the theatre, which holds "a mirror up to nature," might reflect today!

In this rapidly changing world, the theatre is changing too. In June 1969, I was both lifted and uplifted by the inaugural theatre production of the National Arts Centre in Ottawa—a play called *The Ecstasy of Rita Joe* by a brilliant Canadian playwright, George Ryga. The play's theme is the tragic struggle of the Indian, particularly the Indian woman, who too often faces disaster when she moves from the reservation to the perilous adjustments of the big city.

Playwrights today, frantically concerned with breaking forms apparently for breaking's sake, seem pushed into a desperate frenzy. In *The Ecstasy of Rita Joe,* Ryga has succeeded, for the content breaks the form, which is as it should be. I think this work will be recognized someday as one of Canada's first great plays.

But what about the other changes in "modern" theatre? There is a great deal of discussion, pro and con, about bawd and nudity in productions. There is, in my opinion, nothing wrong with bawd when it clarifies by word or action some necessary question in the play. Nor is there anything wrong with nudity, though, personally, I think it more appropriate at the swimming pool or on a beach. But when either bawd or nudity is used to titillate the jaded sensibilities of the overdressed, overfed, and sometimes overdrunk members of an audience, or for profit, it is out of place and should be in some other establishment of the sort usually designated for such entertainment. Dressing actors in their skins seems to be a highly unnecessary, if economical, way of costuming a play, and generally offers nothing more, to my way of thinking, than a curious distraction to any content the play might have.

When human achievements outdistance even the wildest imaginings of the science fiction writers, dislocations in philosophy, manners, and mores must follow, and, inevitably, the theatre reflects these dislocations. The artist sees the present as it is and, in consequence, prophetically, the future in the present. In my time, men have paced across the last frontiers and walked upon the moon. I would be much happier about our achievements if all men were walking "safe and dry shod on the shifting sands" of planet Earth as well.

So I have written this memoir. Some may say I have written with bitterness in places. I can't deny it. What I have recorded are my memories of my life, and it has contained joys, victories, struggles, and defeats. Some of my memories are bitter, and writing of them has been a painful and traumatic experience. It is impossible for me, still, to think of the untimely death of a good and honourable man without bitterness.

There is a Tibetan proverb: "Not to be cheered by praise, not to be grieved by blame, but to know thoroughly one's own virtues or powers are the characteristics of an excellent man." We tried all our lives, Burton and I, not to be overly cheered nor grieved but to achieve excellence in our lives and work.

The experiences of my life, even though they may not all have been ones I would have chosen had I been given the opportunity, have all been *my* experiences, and I am grateful for what they taught me.

Epilogue

RITA SHELTON DEVERELL

Seven decades have passed since Florence Bean James arrived in Regina and her newly adopted Canada to work and live until her last breath. "Mrs. James," as she was most frequently addressed, was then in her early sixties: handsome, fashionable, urbane, a cigarette always in her hand. She'd just come from the United States, which was much richer in things, including sophistication, in 1952.

Canada had always seemed impoverished to Mrs. James. But not now.

> I used to come to Canada and they looked awfully poor to me when I'd come across the border. I used to be glad that my immigrant parents, grandparents, had come to the

> States and not to Canada. I thought that was an advantage.
>
> And I'd never earned any money really for theatre work until I came to Canada, or gotten any recognition for anything—except maybe a jail sentence—anywhere else.*

When Florence immigrated, Saskatchewan did not yet have full electricity. Farming was the largest industry—family farms run by generations of individuals. Most of the small towns did not need or have hotels where a traveller might be put up overnight.

What Saskatchewan *had* though, which was a remarkable achievement, was its Arts Board. In a truly dramatic, historical irony, at the same time the Washington legislature resolved to have an Un-American Activities Committee, Saskatchewan's legislature voted in favour of an Arts Board. Tommy Douglas's Co-operative Commonwealth Federation (CCF), the first social democratic government in North America, had been elected in 1944. In 1948, the CCF proclaimed, as a priority, the Saskatchewan Arts Board to give "the people . . . the opportunity to participate in music, drama, visual arts, handicrafts, and the other arts."

The arts were seen as creating community in a province without a decent auditorium in the capital city. We Canadians had not acknowledged, by the creation

* Florence James in conversation with the author, Regina, 1976–77.

of the Canada Council, that federal subsidy to the arts was a good thing. Saskatchewan saw the light first and put its money on the line.

The James team had made their first appearance in the province in 1950, two years after the board's birth. The board's 1951 *Annual Report* notes their August workshop, and the 1952 *Annual Report* expresses sympathy at Burton's death.* Thereafter, Florence James appears permanently, and alone, in Saskatchewan.

Mrs. James travelled to a huge number of communities geographically and to different communities of interests and skills. All were inspired, all would grow and create, and Florence would perceptively begin her drama teaching at the level of skill each group had. Anything and anybody she touched gained in confidence, purpose, style, awards, and rewards. Who knew they had that much in them?

Florence helped push and shape the centre of the universe—the central cities of Ottawa, Toronto, Montreal, and Stratford—from her outpost in Regina. Perhaps what made the theatre scene in Saskatchewan different from the rest of Canada in the 1950s were three unique assets: the Arts Board, Florence James, and the notion that the arts had social, communal, and political purposes, as well as cultural intent. The amateur/professional divide was not the important one for Florence, Burton,

---

* *Annual Report of the Saskatchewan Arts Board to the Legislature (1951)*, 11; *Annual Report of the Saskatchewan Arts Board to the Legislature (1952)*, 12.

and their Seattle colleagues. The term they used to describe their work was "serious." The work was not approached lightly. This serious attitude, respect for the work and the people who did it, Florence brought to Saskatchewan. She gained the respect of the province's equally serious farmers, teachers, church and synagogue women's auxiliaries, and little theatres.

Florence shared some of the memories of her travels with me more than twenty years later. She didn't drive but travelled by train, and was very proud of her ability to tough out the winters.

> One of the first things, I'd been teaching summer school and there was a young lady there from Carrot River . . . . and she was interested in developing a drama program. I said to Norah [Norah McCullough, then secretary of the Arts Board], "Well I'm off to Carrot River tomorrow."
>
> She said, "Oh do you know what it's like up there? They're having a blizzard. You haven't got a fur coat." And I said, "Listen, I wasn't hired 'weather permitting.'"*

A retired Regina high school teacher, Marge Ziolkowski, was living in Carrot River at the time and remembers Mrs. James's trip. Florence did indeed arrive without a

* Florence James in conversation with the author, Regina, 1976–77.

fur coat. She arrived in a cape. The citizens of the town considered this most dramatic and eccentric. The United Church minister's wife had requested the visit, and the drama workshop was held in the church. Mrs. James, while addressing the group, put her foot up on the pew. The citizens were shocked a second time.

But what is mainly remembered is neither the cape nor the leg on the pew. Mrs. Ziolkowski remembers that Florence took a group of people with no training, with little obvious talent, a stiff group of people, "and did not worry about what they could not do." Mrs. James had every confidence in the Carrot River hardware store owner, high school teacher, and church members. The new drama group was successful and confident after her coaching.

Meanwhile, in the rest of Canada, theatre was much more a gentleman's hobby for the well-off or for those with enough time away from paid jobs to pursue a labour-intensive pastime. Florence shared her "serious" ethic and that helped to drive Canadian theatre toward professionalism. Her distinction was not whether one was paid and therefore professional, or not paid and therefore amateur. Florence's distinction was serious versus froth. Florence was supportive of numerous individuals in civil service and arts positions in Saskatchewan where they could have the same kind of vigorous creative life she had had and was still having. She knew the theatre was a community-building activity and made it possible for professional theatre to find a home in her new province and country.

In 1976, Ken Kramer, one of Globe Theatre's founding artistic directors, asked me to take on the task of recording Florence's life on reel-to-reel audiotape. The two of us met in her small room in Regina's Canadian National Institute for the Blind residence. Hours talking with Florence then mushroomed into numerous taped conversations in Saskatchewan, Ontario, Vancouver, and Seattle with those who knew her life and work.

One of Florence's funnier stories was about moving to Ottawa in the late 1960s after her retirement from the Arts Board. She told me she had to come back to Regina where there was lots going on. Ottawa was dull. There was no National Arts Centre yet. It was a civil service town. Everyone went home at 4:00 p.m. Who would live in a place like that, if they had a choice?

In Saskatchewan, there were theatre performances and rehearsals to watch, tons of music, lectures, and many lively intellectuals with whom to have philosophic arguments. Florence and her Arts Board colleagues had caused Saskatchewan to be a place that Ottawa couldn't rival. With the coming of professional theatre to Saskatoon and the Globe, with its extensive provincial tour from Regina, Florence was given, and could justifiably take, a lot of credit.

The interviews I recorded in the 1970s and '80s with Florence's colleagues, friends, and family made a huge impression on me. They also helped me to understand how the woman I met when she was elderly and somewhat frail had been a force of nature in people's lives, careers, and communities. The people I spoke with had met Florence in the long prime time of her life, and it was as if they got an electrical jolt that stayed with them. Florence James is remembered for her forceful personality, strong character, great intellectual, moral, and artistic courage, and the imprint she left on others.

> Florence was more than happy to come to us because . . . she got away from all this poison and friends had fallen away. Not only that, her trial had cost her an awful lot of money, something like thirty-five thousand dollars. They were bankrupt.
>
> And it was sort of hopeless, opportunities in Seattle. Nobody was going to dare engage them.
>
> She was erased . . . . It was kind of an honour, wasn't it, to be convicted by that crowd of thugs?*

In Saskatchewan, too, the Recreational and Cultural Survey of the State of Washington, conducted by the

* Norah McCullough, former executive secretary, Saskatchewan Arts Board, in conversation with the author, Guelph, Ontario, 1988.

Jameses and their son-in-law, Jack Kinzel, surfaced as possibly subversive. According to Norah McCullough, this survey, which went to the people to ask them their needs and organized communities to solve their own problems, only later to be questioned by the Un-American Activities Committee, brought its controversial history with it. Saskatchewan's Education Minister Woodrow Lloyd was disturbed by the rumours he'd heard about the Jameses and the survey's resulting report, *Recreation for All.*

> Woodrow drove me home and he said, "I want to ask you about Florence James and her husband. Do you think they were Communists?"
>
> I said, "I don't think so." And he said, "Well, it seems they were harassed in Seattle because of their left-wing tendencies and because of a proposal he made to the government at that time" . . . And he said, "Do you know what the proposal was?" And I said, "Yes, I've got a copy."
>
> So I trotted into my little house on Rose Street and found this and took it out to him. And he sat in the car and he read over the thing. And he said, "Well, it sounds like the Saskatchewan Arts Board."
>
> And I said, "Yes, exactly."*

* Norah McCullough, former executive secretary, Saskatchewan Arts Board, in conversation with the author, Guelph, Ontario, 1988.

What had been such a controversial idea in Seattle was a welcomed idea in Saskatchewan. David Smith, the civil servant who designed the Saskatchewan Arts Board, understood the place of an arts board in their new society.

> Adult education in a socialist society . . . is highly participatory . . . . In other words, we were a democratic one in which the citizens make the decisions and determine the policies and determine the program.
>
> It also is a society that values human ingenuity and capacity and creativity . . . The purpose of it is full realization or development of these capacities . . . and, of course, . . . notions about equality.
>
> Well, an Arts Board, one of the things that people do . . . is to sing and write and sculpt and model and do all these kinds of artistic activities, so an Arts Board indeed is a way of mobilizing the citizen capacities and creativity wherever it may happen to be.*

Observers of the Jameses' theatre over time were not gripped by the spectacle. They were not gripped by the staging. What mesmerized them was the intellectual

---

* David Smith, former head of Adult Education Department, Saskatchewan, in conversation with the author, Barrie, Ontario, 1988.

focus of the acting and the clarity and meaning of the text. Audiences and theatre people alike were attracted by the strength, not the entertainment, of the work.

When Florence Bean James came to Saskatchewan in the 1950s, she created performances that made a lasting and profound impression. And she was at the height of her career. Upon her death, Mavor Moore, the revered arts journalist, producer, and one of Florence's fellow Canadian Theatre Centre board members, had this to say in the *Globe and Mail* on February 13, 1988:

> THEATRE PIONEER WAS A WELCOME U.S. INVADER
>
> "The world will not be saved on the political, military or economic level but on the level of education and art."
> —*Saskatchewan Theatre Pioneer*
> *Florence James (1892–1988)*
>
> In Regina tomorrow they will be holding a memorial event for Florence Bean James. She died Jan. 18 at the age of 95. Although she was already past 60 when she arrived in Saskatchewan from Seattle, the news of her death merited a full-page obituary in *The Regina Leader-Post.* But outside of the theatre community, and outside of the West, it appears to have gone unnoticed—perhaps because

we've paid very little attention to the phenomenon she personified: the benign American invasion of Canada that accompanied the McCarthy years in the United States.

Florence James was one of the most remarkable of a small group of remarkable women who bullied the performing arts in this country into professionalism, not because she believed in art for art's sake but because she believed the arts have a job to do. She once quoted to me James Baldwin's remark, "Life is more important than art, that's what makes art so important." Born in Idaho and trained in Boston and New York as [an] actor, director and playwright, she reversed the trend and came to Canada to fulfill her ambition. Her ambition was to make human beings, not money.

. . . She was godmother to the now nationally important Globe Theatre, and to generations of young people who learned to share her social conscience and her love of theatre as its crucible. . . .

There will be those today who see the Florence Jameses as political infiltrators bent on subverting our youth, just as the burghers of Seattle did . . . They miss the point that she and others like her grasped: that if you

> want to build human beings, you start with their humanity, not with their color, sex, class, consumer status or political persuasion. You build a society in which humanity can grow . . . Then you keep working at it, through education and art, until you die.

A scan of the contemporary scene suggests we still can reach out in our time, in different ways, toward what Florence James and the Saskatchewan Arts Board accomplished from 1950 to 1980. The mere existence of professional arts, supported by the government—Florence would never have seen that as the highest pinnacle of achievement.

Professional arts, rather, are an option that an enlightened society owes those with the talent and inclination the opportunity to pursue. From Florence's philosophic vantage point, there are four areas in particular where we still have work to do. First, she had a philosophy of casting beyond race, accent, or other traditional barriers for which many still strive in Canada.

> There's no distinction. When talent emerges, whether it's Black or white or any other colour, it's there. It's completely integrated.
>
> When talent emerges, it doesn't make any difference what colour it is. This is the strangest thing—that somehow or other in

> my generation and your generation that you had to learn that there isn't any distinction.*

Second, the extensive theatre tours, especially to young people "throughout the length and breadth" of the province, have almost disappeared. Third, there are fewer plays created and produced by, for, and about Saskatchewan and its issues. And, finally, the arts now are less participatory, less inclusive, and less available to all sorts and conditions of women, men, and children.

Florence Bean James made Saskatchewan stronger, the arts in Saskatchewan and all of Canada tougher. And the many, many individuals and communities that were touched by her standards, her ensemble, her creative drive, can still reach forward to do what else needs to be done.

And, rightly, the last words belong to Florence herself:

> Remembering was a very traumatic experience. But somehow we survived. We survived.
>
> And one of the marvellous things—was this ensemble that we had. Every one of those people suffered in one way or another, either by being interviewed by FBI agents or by their parents who wanted them to get away from the Playhouse and forget the whole thing and

* Florence James in conversation with the author, Regina, 1976–77.

hope to goodness they wouldn't be caught up in it.

Not one ever appeared as a witness against us. Tyrone Guthrie in his book makes a point: He said if you have an ensemble in the theatre nothing else matters. He said if you haven't . . . it doesn't matter what your subsidy is or your glamour, you have to have an ensemble—and they stuck.

I'll tell you something else, Rita, I always got from my father. Two things that I'll never forget: Pay your bills, don't run bills.

And the other thing is: Stand up for what you believe. And it was never any effort for me when I felt that I was right to stand up for what I thought and express myself. And instead of killing me it made me tougher.*

* Florence James in conversation with the author, Regina, 1976–77.

Appendix 1:

FLORENCE BEAN JAMES ON ACTING

I long ago rejected the idea that acting was something that could not be taught. For centuries, actors have tried to understand, even to codify, the processes by which they learned their craft and developed their art. The imaginative powers of the actor and his craftsmanship are completely dependent on each other.

Sometimes it seems to me that successful artists have done as much mischief in this area as anyone, perpetuating the myth of the rarely endowed, the "unique soul." Perhaps their struggles have been so painful, so arduous, they have come to feel their position, however secure, must be the result of efforts beyond themselves, of the supernatural. Or perhaps they simply wish to discourage competition! Konstantin Stanislavski and his followers attempted to perfect a method to create by will conditions favourable for the appearance of inspiration, but, as theatre critic George Henry Lewes once said, "Trusting to the inspiration of the moment is like trusting to a shipwreck for your first lesson in swimming."*

Many actors and directors learned their craft by watching other actors and directors at work. My own experience in the theatre has always involved me in the teaching process. My first directing was of amateurs, and amateurs have to be trained. I brought the same attitude to this activity that I did to directing—however effective I might be, I never knew enough and always wanted to spend time exploring new approaches and techniques. I never gave up my quest. Never!

I think my philosophy of actor training begins with an essential belief in the potential creativity of anyone who has ever approached me seeking the opportunity to do this work. I knew nothing of the capacities of the twenty-five Black people who came to the Playhouse one Sunday afternoon for the first reading of Paul Green's *In Abraham's Bosom*. When it came to casting the play, I had to judge their capacities, aptitudes—in essence, whatever had brought them there. What brought them there was the urge to do something they had possibly wanted to do all their lives. I recognized their essential creativity and never doubted my ability to open that "horrible, horrible cage, that utterly horrible cage"—as

---

* Lewes, George Henry. *On Actors and the Art of Acting*. New York: Henry Holt and Company, 1878, 97.

Vincent van Gogh once described it—that imprisoned the creative urge.

This urge, this aptitude, is essentially what a person is born with—the mental, nervous, and muscular abilities that fit someone for a given activity, such as acting. This inheritance can grow by being developed or deteriorate by being neglected or mistrained. To this degree, it is subject to teaching and experience, but its quality and degree vary from person to person. It is a native attribute of the individual and cannot be taught into existence. It can only be built upon.

The other element of the actor's ability or urge can be taught and can be developed by use and experience—technique. I think it is clear you cannot make a good or gifted actor out of everybody. While the native aptitudes of many individuals are much higher than most people suspect, and certainly high enough to make an actor of sorts out of almost anyone of "normal" faculties, the level of proficiency will still differ greatly from person to person.

There is a third element that belongs in this formula—opportunity. And this, it seems to me, may be the most important element, for without opportunity (access to training and a chance to use skills), neither aptitude nor technique is of much use.

When I started my work at Lenox Hill, I was dealing with a group of young people who wanted to act in plays. I had rejected the techniques I had learned at Emerson but knew of no other approaches to actor training. I had, however, acquired an excellent background in literature at Emerson, and our classes in interpretation had provided insight into the meanings and intentions of the author. And I had learned, through the scenes and plays I worked on in college, how to develop stage action. So I read the script of whatever play we were working on carefully, including stage directions given by the author. For the rest, I had to depend on intuition, an instinctive sensitivity to the actor's needs—and a great enthusiasm for the task.

Very few books or studies on actor training were available to help me with my problems until Louis Calvert's *Problems of the Actor*, published in 1918, came to hand. Calvert's book did not give specific directions but outlined the essentials that I, working in the dark, needed to carve out techniques I would find useful. These were humanity, a real interest in people, imagination, enthusiasm, and a sense of humour.

In 1936, the first article in the first issue of *Theatre Workshop*, a quarterly magazine that dealt with all phases of theatrical activity, gave me my first definite answers. The article was by Josef Rapoport, who had studied with Stanislavski and had worked in the Moscow Art Theatre. Rapoport confines the first exercises to the five senses—sight, touch, smell, hearing, and taste. For the first, sight, I used an antique silver Chinese bracelet I had had for years and which is on my wrist as I write this. The bracelet consists of seven frames, in each of which is a Chinese flower or leaves. I asked each student in turn to look at the bracelet. To begin with, no one actually looked at it; instead, they acted out "looking." Without exception, they tried it on, waved it about, and really saw nothing. I called a student back and said, "Identify the plant in that particular frame of the bracelet." At once, he concentrated on the one frame, all tension gone in the process of accomplishing the task. He was not trying to do something about the task—he was doing it.

The smell and taste exercises provided interesting experiences too. I used saucers of brown liquids—black coffee, soy sauce, Worcestershire sauce, vanilla. All looked the same, but all had different smells and tastes. For hearing, we listened to our own breathing, then all the sounds in the room, then outside the room, then every sound that could be heard anywhere—birds, planes, dogs barking, and so on. For touch, I gave them a piece of material while their eyes were closed and asked them to determine what the material was—its texture, length, shape, quality. A student once asked me, referring to the many kinds of exercises we did, "This is acting?" I replied, "Not quite. But it's the beginning, and everything you are doing is a stage task."

Once, on a tour of Thornton Wilder's *Our Town*, a local fireman had to sit on the stage near what was to be imagined as the kitchen door of the Gibbs's house, which, of course, in *Our Town* isn't really there. Every time the actress playing the part of Mrs. Gibbs opened that imaginary door, the fireman moved his legs, as if he thought they might be in the road of the door, so complete was the actress's action. The fireman's reaction was a source of amused satisfaction to us.

When I first started teaching the Playhouse classes, I gave the students themes to develop into scenes. They started with dialogue and had soon talked themselves out of both steam and believability. I changed my approach and gave a student three unrelated activities, such as counting money, taking off a shoe, and using a Kleenex, to build a stage action. Then I paired students, each with three different activities. They had a few minutes to decide who they were, what their relationship was, and where they were. They had to find justification for each activity separately then link them in one general justification. They found these justifications through their imagination. All artists must have a rich imagination, actors especially, for they are entirely surrounded by fictions, make-believe, which they must endow with believability. Every movement, even a glance, a pause, must have a justification derived from a true-life situation, projected by memory, enriched by imagination.

Sarah Bernhardt said, "An actor must be—if not a scholar or a learned man—at least what used to be called an 'all-round man'; that is, he should not be inferior in the manner of acquired knowledge to the average of mankind." This acquired knowledge enables an actor to project himself, through his imagination, into the consciousness of another human being and the situation in which he finds himself.

All our actors participated in our workshops. Working with other directors and teachers, I learned to use music to establish situations: you are walking barefoot on hot cement, soft grass, a sandy beach, deep mud, in a blizzard, across a flimsy bridge over a deep chasm. These exercises were especially helpful in handling a large group, for each student could find his own experience unobserved by others. When I had problems in directing plays, I devised improvisations in the workshops to solve them. We frequently improvised scenes the author of the play had not included in the script but which had to have taken place.

In 1951, I came across an article by Mao Tse-tung in the British magazine, *Labour Monthly*. In the article, called "Concerning Practice: The Connection between Cognition and Practice," Mao noted that some knowledge is known only empirically, that is, through study, experiment, and experience. "The first step in the process of cognition is contact with the external environment, the stage of sensations, that is, sense perceptions." (I like the word "cognition," used interchangeably with the word "knowledge," for it seems to have an extension that "knowledge" lacks.) "The second step is the summing-up of the materials of sense perceptions, setting in order—and rearrangement—the stage of concepts, judgments, and inferences, the development of theories, the application of rational knowledge. The important third step is practice, without which no theory, no matter how good it may be, can have significance."

When actor and teacher accept the conditions of their work, eliminate superficial, mystical thinking, and call on history, science, philosophy, and literature to aid them in their efforts, realizing that the stage of sensations with which they begin their work is undoubtedly a reflection of the reality of the existing world—that sensations can be understood and evaluated, and serve as a basis for rational knowledge, and that theories of work can be developed and tested in practice—they can then evolve an approach to the learning process of the actor.

If student actors realize they are learning to do a job governed by certain laws that can be investigated and used, and that accurate results can be achieved, confidence returns and with it that special condition, the "creative mood," without which no creativity is possible. And having found it once, students can learn how to find it again and again.

Appendix 2:

FLORENCE BEAN JAMES ON DIRECTING

Directing seems to require a Superman (or perhaps a Wonder Woman!). The director must be energetic, enthusiastic, inspiring, authoritative (yet not didactic or autocratic), impartial, fair, honest, stable, reliable, and firm. On the other hand, he or she must be gentle, human, tactful, and diplomatic in the extreme. The director must be discreet, dignified, and cautious (but not superior or haughty), patient, tolerant, understanding, broadminded, open to suggestion, wise, progressive, and intuitive. Few positions require such contrasting qualities. A director must be idealistic yet practical. A director must have business sense and training.

This creature has emerged as a defined entity only in the last half-century. In the past, there must have been someone in the player group who put the thing together, someone who moved the actors about the stage, "kept them from bumping into each other," made decisions about scenery, costumes, lights, etc. Leading actors often did not rehearse with the cast and sometimes did not see them until opening night.

I remember well when and why I became a director: there were always more women than men in any theatre group I was associated with. Someone had to take charge, and I was available, not being needed on stage. *How* I became a director, I don't quite know. At Emerson, the greatest emphasis was on interpretation. In our senior and postgraduate years, we were required to produce scenes from plays. We never received any instruction in how to go about this but managed to get them lighted, costumed, and on the boards.

I think the reluctance to teach theatre skills must have been the result of the puritanical attitude toward theatre so prevalent then. Emerson was careful to avoid being identified as a training school for theatre. The Boston Theatre had once circumvented the Puritan-propagated suspicion of the stage's moral propriety by calling itself a "Museum and Gallery of Fine Arts." One floor was stocked with monstrosities, mummies, and some pictures, and performances given in the "spacious music hall" above were called "moral dissertations." *Othello*, for instance, conveniently became an "uplifting colloquy on the evils of jealousy."

It was at Emerson that I first found myself in the position of a director, though in all probability the term hadn't even been coined then. Robert Frost's collection of poems *North of Boston* had just been published and included a poem called "The Death of the Hired Man." Frost wanted to see how this dramatic poem would work when staged and approached the school for a group of young actors to play in it. I don't remember whether I was assigned to it or, always keen for adventure, volunteered. But I remember very well the excitement of working with young Mr. Frost, who ran up and down the aisle of our auditorium, helping us make his poem into a play.

When we came to cast it, all our available male students seemed too young for the part of the husband. One day, Thomas Watson appeared—perhaps Frost persuaded him to come. This was the same Thomas Watson who had worked with Alexander Graham Bell in the creation of the telephone, the first person to hear and answer the thing when Mr. Bell, calling from another room, said, "Come here, Watson. I want you." Mr. Watson was a very nice elderly gentleman, infinitely patient with my fumbling efforts to direct him. The production pleased all of us but didn't seem to have stimulated Robert Frost to become a playwright, although the dialogue in his poems talks.

When the opportunity to direct presented itself, I had some knowledge of plays acquired at Emerson and a way with people. I was energetic and enthusiastic and able to create excitement around a project. And I seemed to the actors to know what I was doing. But who and what is a director? I had an empirical approach to the problems of directing, and I knew it—what worked was right. But what to do when something did not work! I recognized my limitations and constantly worked and studied to find more definitive answers to my problems. I read and reread a number of books, but I found them confusing, to say the least. They emphasized the need for what seemed to me to be the various elements of the well-produced play and then provided arbitrary, mechanical devices for achieving them.

I was in the favourable position of being able to apply and practise as I studied, for from Cornish School days on I was constantly involved in directing a play or plays; later, at the Playhouse and the university, two and sometimes three at the same time. It seemed to me that even if all the devices suggested in the books could be understood and applied, a director would still be far from his objective—a well-produced play.

The confusion of opinions merely emphasized the comparative newness of our struggles to better understand our medium and to try to formulate laws governing the process. Our attempts were so new that we had difficulty understanding each other, for there was no precise, generally acceptable terminology. In my early experiences as a director, I studied the play and lectured to the cast on the author's biography and intention in writing the play, the meaning of the play, and so on. Later, at the Playhouse, I demanded that the actors do this research and bring their insights and opinions, based on knowledge derived from their study, to our reading rehearsals and play analyses. Before this, I had done a great deal of demonstration to stir the actors' imaginations, suggesting appropriate action. I later found this approach a waste of time. A director who demonstrates badly does little or nothing to stimulate the actor, and a director who demonstrates well frustrates the actor. I once saw a two-hundred-pound man galumphing about the stage to show a fourteen-year-old girl how to come in "like a summer breeze."

When we had our own theatre, and a group of people working in it who were dedicated to development and growth, we had opportunities to experiment with theories and test results. These people, including members of the staff and others who looked on the theatre as an avocation, spent long hours in discussion and classes. Our thinking led us to some very definite conclusions: acting and directing can be learned, given aptitude for this kind of work. There are unknowns but no unknowables. We believed the process of learning to act was a knowable, get-at-able process, that failures and successes encountered in the process could be judged and evaluated every step of the way.

Where and what is the director in this process? Alexander Dean says the director is an interpretative artist, while the playwright and the actor are creative artists. I disagree. I believe the result of the creative efforts of all three interprets the author's intention and the play's meaning for the audience, who in turn participate in creatively interpreting for themselves the significant meanings of the play. Any work of art shapes, forms, and develops feelings, influences thinking and beliefs, and actively assists in the process of transforming life.

To say that it makes no difference whether the feelings engendered or thoughts stimulated by a work of art benefit or improve humankind is to say that a work of art is a thing apart from life. We work in art, and art in us, for the betterment or detriment of each. Hitler's dictum of what was good art for Germany became bad for both Germany and art. He was able to destroy in a relatively short time the great creativity of a nation that had produced Goethe, Beethoven, Mendelssohn, and Schiller, and in his own day Reinhardt and Brecht.

The director's creativity is no less than that of the playwright or actor. As the director reads the play, he or she hears the lines spoken, sees the colour of the costumes, the movements and attitudes of the characters, and the general feeling and mood of the whole thing. The director's concept of the play stimulates the imagination of the scene designers, costume designers, makeup people, electricians, and even more, the actors. Every detail of a production is in the director's hands. A very practical attitude toward budgets is required, as well as a complete knowledge of how to get what is needed and, if that cannot be obtained, how to achieve the desired end with what is available. I have never found that working on a budget, no matter how limited, really deterred me from my objective.

Once, when we were producing Albert Bein's *Heavenly Express*, the scene designer was dressing the set and called me in to look at it. I said, "It's good, all but the curtains. They're too clean." The set was the interior of a boarding house near a railroad, catering to trainmen and tramps. In the day of the coal-fired engine, curtains in such a location would never be clean and fresh. I said, "Get that carton of old curtains out of the prop storeroom." Somebody had donated a box of worn, ragged drapes, and it had been duly put away until it would be required. The scene designer objected to my choice. "But those are faded and filthy." I said, "Let's hang them and see." We did. The curtains were faded and filthy but right—not only right but beautiful, with the light shining through them.

It was our practice, after the play was cast and in first rehearsals, to have what we called "reading rehearsals" for ten days to two weeks. Scene designers, costume designers, and actors participated, and it was in these rehearsals that the designers, before they put pencil to paper, became completely aware of the dimensions of their problems.

In the commercial theatre, where the director and actors are hastily assembled, time for rehearsals is limited—four to six weeks at most—so long reading rehearsals such as we enjoyed would not be possible. For one thing, prohibitive costs for actors' salaries would prevent it. But we had a closely unified group of people who had worked together for months or years, and we found these rehearsals saved time and increased cohesion. No one felt incidental to the effort, or that being cast in a small part meant they were unimportant.

In our reading rehearsals, we did an analysis of the play, helping us to understand and place subjective and objective work in their proper relationship. What do I mean by "subjective and objective work"? Subjective work involves the study of the play as a whole and, if it is a classic of the magnitude of Goethe's *Faust* or Ibsen's *Peer Gynt*, a study of the author himself, his period, his life. For these two plays, the director and the main actors spent months preparing. We also had to prepare the playing script, and this cannot be done haphazardly. An analysis of a play greatly facilitated this work, and we were able to get what you might call a blueprint—the author's intention in writing the play, its theme, the author's success or failure in developing his theme, and the selection and use made of character and situation. I remember very well Irwin Shaw's horrified exclamation over an analysis we made of his play, *The Gentle People*. His comment was "How can you act a play when you tear it to pieces? Doesn't this kind of work destroy your inspiration?"

We didn't believe it did. We were bringing our thinking to bear on the problems so inspiration could flow more freely and from a sound base. I don't think it is dangerous to a production for a director to understand the social framework of the play, the thinking of the author that suggested the theme, and the author's treatment of the theme in all its strengths and weaknesses. I have directed plays for which the author had written no climax, made the climax an offstage noise, or even written an altogether different climax than his theme, character, and situation demanded, perhaps because he (or, horrible to contemplate, the play doctor) thought it more dramatic.

Recognizing these problems early in the rehearsal is a help rather than a hindrance. After all, inspiration is no gossamer thing that will vanish if scrutinized but rather the result of a number of things, not excluding a lot of hard work. Inspiration is the synthesis of many elements and is achieved as a result of complete analysis, which clears the way.

During this period of rehearsal, actors were able to visualize their characters, feel them, hear them, see them, and find justification for their activities and attitudes. I think of this as a period of germination, or gestation if you prefer. We were particularly careful to read and understand the author's stage directions and whatever descriptions were given of characters and the situation in which they were put. In a well-written play, the descriptions and directions are vastly important to the meaning and development of the play. I dare anyone to overlook or ignore one of Anton Chekhov's directions.

Actors fail when the subjective work is neglected or overlooked, or when their skills are insufficient or their abilities to objectify or translate in terms of action are undeveloped. Too often the director or actor concentrates on externals, what we called in our theatre "playing results." No amount of direction, such as "take the speech faster" or "you haven't got the mood," will produce right results. I don't direct "results"—this scene is joyful, that scene is gloomy. These results must be achieved in direction. A mood is a result.

At the Playhouse, we saw first-hand how an actor's incorrect approach to a speech not only put a scene off but affected the last two acts of a play. We were producing William Saroyan's *The Time of Your Life,* which is written in five acts. We broke for a long intermission at the end of the third act, and the play resumed with the policeman making a longish speech to Nick the bartender. The opening of the fourth act just wasn't working. It killed the last two acts. After watching the performances for several evenings, I questioned the actor playing the policeman. He was very sympathetic to the character he portrayed, was impressed with the speech, and loved the scene.

So we went back to the analysis. What were the events of this particular day? Why had he come into the bar? Where had he come from? We established that the policeman is on duty on the waterfront because his friend the longshoreman is on strike. His relief arrives, so he comes to Nick's bar for a glass of beer. He knows Nick, likes and trusts him. On this particular day, the head of the vice squad has decided to get a little publicity for the coming election by persecuting prostitutes. The policeman hates this man and the vice squad. As he enters Nick's bar, he meets two prostitutes who are impudent to him simply because he is a policeman and they identify him with all their persecutors. At this point, the policeman, with the glass of beer he can't enjoy, "blows his top" to Nick. He came to the bar not to make speeches but to find relaxation in a glass of beer. Simple as that is, it is spoiled for him, and his speech, an angry protest, results. Once he understood all this, the actor playing the policeman realized he had been simply delivering a speech and changed his interpretation. The scene and, consequently, the play, changed. Tempo—always a result—increased. Movement developed, meaning was revealed, and the extension necessary to the dynamic development of the play toward its climax and conclusion was achieved.

A graphic example of a director's failure to define his objective, which led to his failure in directing an actor in his task, was once given me by a prominent Hollywood director at Warner Brothers. I was watching, with considerable interest, the shooting of a scene for a movie, the name of which I probably never did know. Shortly after shooting started, word came from the front office that Mr. Warner had seen the rushes of a scene shot the previous day and didn't like them. The director immediately dropped the scene he was working on. Props, lights, cameras, and sound trucks were rearranged for retakes on the previous day's scene. While all this was going on, no one bothered to ask (nor was the information volunteered) just *what* Mr. Warner didn't like about the first version. It was enough that he didn't like it.

When the actor got into place, the director said, "Now, Mr. Gardiner, make this good." I cannot imagine a direction less likely to get "something good" out of an actor. Good for what? In this case, it was to be good for the front office.

It is important, rewarding, and simplifies larger problems of directors and actors to use the actual props and complete activities suggested by the play early in the rehearsals. Earlier in my directing experience, I permitted actors to pantomime such activities in the earlier rehearsals, often with painful results at dress rehearsals.

When a character is developed around given activities, as, for example, Eddie mixing drinks in Garson Kanin's *Born Yesterday*, I had fairly exact replicas of the glasses and bottles he would be using, complete with liquid (nonalcoholic, of course) contents. These were provided early in the rehearsals. The actor then has no major adjustments to make in switching to somewhat more elaborate bottles, glasses, and bar appointments in the actual production, because he is accustomed to using approximately the same thing in rehearsals.

I never really understood why a well-rehearsed play could go to pieces at dress rehearsal until I read the story of Dr. Pavlov and his dogs and his findings on the conditioned reflex. I then realized that preparatory rehearsals were a kind of conditioning, and I had been changing the equations at dress rehearsals. I found it helpful to the actors to provide proper conditioning to stage tasks, with props, costumes, trains, hoop skirts, swords, canes, and so on, as early as possible in the stage rehearsals, so there would be as few adjustments as possible needed in the dress rehearsals.

In the last act of *The Diary of Anne Frank*, Mr. Frank, the only person in the group to survive the death camps, returns to the garret where he and his family and friends had lived for so many bitter months. When I directed this scene, all I could get from the actor playing Mr. Frank was an entrance from backstage. He brought nothing with him. So, at one rehearsal, I put all the other characters on stage in places where he would remember them to have been. Mr. Frank entered and looked at them, one after another. At a gesture from me, they quietly left the scene. When Mr. Frank saw the diary and Anne's white glove on the floor, picked them up, and began to speak, the scene had the necessary emotional impact. After rehearsal, the actor said to me, "My God, a trick like that made my blood run cold!" A trick, perhaps, but it stimulated his imagination and triggered an emotional response we both wanted.

When an actor enters the scene with the subjective work already done, the mere action of stepping into the scene begins the step-by-step process of the character's development. This development changes and grows as it is objectified. As this work is not being done only by the actor but is a collective effort involving the cast and the director, transformation of the actor into the character is possible, inevitable, and the play is translated from literature into theatre.

When the synthesis is really complete—play, actor, and audience—you have that much-to-be-hoped-for result, an inspired performance. I emphasize the audience, for more times than I can recount, I have come backstage after a performance to express my satisfaction and pleasure at the evening's work, and when I say, "Excellent tonight," the response is always "Wonderful audience!" A "Dionysian unity" had been achieved with the audience, that important entity in a living theatre, about which so little is known scientifically.

About the Contributors

JEAN FREEMAN is a celebrated performer and author whose career has spanned radio, television, film, live performance, public relations, and a wide range of writing, including plays and children's books. Perhaps best known for her role on the hit TV series *Corner Gas,* her literary skills and love of drama led to a devoted friendship with Florence B. James.

RITA SHELTON DEVERELL is a theatre artist, academic, journalist, co-founder of VisionTV, Regina resident from 1971 to 1989, and has in development a feature film about Florence James based on her full-length play *McCarthy and the Old Woman,* first produced in 2010.

SEAN PRPICK is the trade editor at University of Regina Press. Prior to entering the publishing industry, Sean, like Jean Freeman, worked for many years with CBC in Saskatchewan and did similar work to hers by finding programming for the national radio network.

A NOTE ABOUT THE TYPE

This book is set in Meridien. It was developed in the mid-1950s and released by the French foundry Deberny & Peignot in 1957. After studying a typeface from the sixteenth century, the Swiss designer Adrian Frutiger was inspired to create an alphabet without any completely straight strokes, and he hoped the reader of a text set in this typeface would feel as though wandering through a forest. The designer of more than 100 typefaces, Frutiger considers Meridien to be his best. With its slightly flared stems and triangular shaped serifs, Meridien is at once sharp, graceful, arresting, and sensuous, much like a forest.

THE REGINA COLLECTION

Named as a tribute to Saskatchewan's capital city with its rich history of boundary-defying innovation, *The Regina Collection* builds upon University of Regina Press's motto of "a voice for many peoples." Intimate in size and beautifully packaged, these books aim to tell the stories of those who have been caught up in social and political circumstances beyond their control.

To see other books in *The Regina Collection* visit www.uofrpress.ca